We Heal our Pets ~ They Heal Us
Together We Heal The World!

1-6-21

Mel

Artist - Melanie Colligan

"The greatness of a nation and its moral progress can be judged by the way its animals are treated."
- Mahatma Gandhi

HEAL WITH YOUR PETS

Authors:

Patti Anastasia RN

Pet Psychic-Medium, Reiki Master,

Medical Intuitive

Ladybug

Spirit Animal Guide & Reiki Master

ANASTASIA'S
HEALTH HAPPENINGS
BLENDING THE MEDICAL WITH THE SPIRITUAL

Contributors:

- Ladybug Anastasia - Co-Author
- Sharoline Galva – Photographer
- Lenore Garnhum – Illustrator
- Katherine Adegoke – Editor and Formatter

Library of Congress Card Number: 2024909373
ISBN: 979-8-9906825-1-1

DEDICATION

Gratitude From Patti

"To all the animals who have shared their love, messages, and their humans with me!"

A special thanks to Putzi my protector, Pepe my connector, Snowflake my cat-dog, Machen my matriarch, Mr. Bo Jangles my serenity, Moochie my mate, Samantha my magic cat, Sadie my miracle girl, Sierra my gift from God, and Ladybug my guide and partner in the physical and spiritual world.

Gratitude From Ladybug

"To all the animals and humans who let me help them heal and who have helped me heal too!"

A special thanks to Mary for connecting me and my Mama, Grandmama for treats and love! Auntie Cheryl and Uncle John for your friendship and love. Melanie, and Nancy for the awesome pictures! Charlie... my boyfriend, Dr. Downey, and my mom's friend Karen, and everyone else at the office for helping me stay healthy and for helping my mom stop worrying!

To the Doctors and helpers in the big building, thank you so much for saving my life and taking such good care of me when I had emergencies! (Bulger Veterinary Hospital).

Love you, Mama and Dada!

Heal With Your Pets!

Table of Contents

If you have any difficulties scanning the QR codes in this book, the links are listed at the end of this book. Please reach out to me at YourAnimalHealer@ gmail.com for any needed assistance

Meet the Author

Enjoy this brief video biography and find out what you can expect in the following pages!

Use your camera to scan the QR code to explore the information

PREFACE

What if you could understand what your pets wanted?

Hi, my name is Patti Anastasia, and I was born with the ability to talk with animals and Spirits. I believe that there is a **Universal Language**, and we all already know it. Sometimes, we just need to be reminded, and our pets can help us do that. It's my goal to help people, animals, and Mother Earth communicate more clearly so we can all heal together.

I was born in 1966 and learned pretty quickly talking with Spirits and animals was crazy to most people. I told my neighborhood friends—who told their parents—that my dog Putzi showed me how to cross the street safely. I even showed them how to do it, too, just like Putzi taught me. Well, you can probably imagine how well that went over!

As I grew up, I realized that the chances of using my natural skills of being a psychic-medium and animal communicator to make a living were slim and full of judgment. I could become a physic-medium-on-the-corner, join a circus, travel with fairs, or find the people who secretly wanted my services.

So, I decided to enter the medical field instead. I felt that by helping people with trauma, in crisis, and with chronic conditions, I could make a difference and have a stable career that I enjoyed.

I became a Massage and Acupressure Therapist in 1994, and then soon after began my 16-year career as an EMT/Paramedic. I decided to return to school to become a nurse, and I worked as a Visiting Nurse in the community for many years.

I saw many types of wounds both physical and emotional. I wanted to do more to help, so I went back to school. I received my master's degree in Wound, Ostomy, and Continence Nursing (WOCN) in 2014.

Whenever I saw my clients and patients, their animals would always "talk" to me, and sometimes, I would share what they said. However, most of the time, I did not.

Throughout my medical career, I had a few Spiritual mentors, like Lazarus and Louise Hay, and I progressively moved in a more Spiritual direction. In 2015, I completed my Reiki training that began in 2004 and became a Holy Fire® III Karuna® Reiki Master. It seemed to be a Spiritual healing method that was more accepted in public.

I started to realize how much the Spiritual community in the World was changing. There was a whole new group of people out there that were embracing (and not judging) the psychic-mediums and the animal communicators around them. They were looking for and were open to their services.

Sometimes, I laugh at myself because I hid behind my medical training so I could be accepted and not judged. Because of that, I missed getting to know many of the wonderful healers and teachers who were breaking ground around me. People still ask me if I know this person or that person, and I mostly say no.

As a dyslexic psychic, I am not naturally a "book-reader," so it takes most of my time to learn something new. I had to pick and choose what to spend my time doing and learning. I wanted to have healthcare benefits, afford to buy things, and to go on vacations. I also wanted financial stability, and I could not see how to do that with a career where I use my natural abilities. I did not reach out to learn about others in the intuitive fields because of the time and energy it would require me to do so -- all my energy was being used to manage the career I chose.

Soon after completing my Reiki master training in 2015, I had an injury that ended my nursing career. My thumbs were already damaged from the years of massage work I did, and I then slipped and fell right on my left thumb. It needed surgical repair. I haven't been able to use my hands well since that accident – except when I'm talking... *ha-ha-ha*.

I decided it was time to embrace my psychic-medium roots and use my natural abilities to help people and animals. I believe that Spirit "kicked" me out of my careers in the medical field so I could do my Spiritual healing work.

I naturally started to blend the Medical with the Spiritual. It was during this transition that I learned that I was a Medical Intuit because I could "see" what was going on in people and animals. Medical Intuit—I didn't know there was a word for this before.

Later, in 2015, I opened a Spiritual Center in Amesbury, MA. I offered Reiki treatments and training, along with crystal and sound therapies. I also offered group meditations and healings, including Spirit-Guided New Moon and Full Moon healings. Ladybug, my dog, was with me most of the time, helping me teach and heal during private sessions. And I loved doing online Gemstone Readings on Facebook for people and animals.

I invited guest speakers and offered psychic fairs for the community. I also had a store with local artists, crystals, and various toolkits for space clearing, chakra healing, and pet communication. I took people on Spiritual Healing field trips to America's Stonehenge and offered fire ceremonies when space was available.

When I started my Spiritual Healing business, animals would stop me on the road while I was driving. They would tell me to let them bring their humans to me. They wanted me to continue my healing offerings to them.

I really could not figure out what this meant or how to market this. Being a dyslexic psychic, I can say the opposite of what I want to. It took me time to develop the right language to communicate well with others, and it can still be a challenge! This is why this book came to be. I hope that it will clarify my words. **I want to tell people about their pets and what I have learned their pets want them to know.**

Although I do continue to work with people, I've found that many people are more comfortable exploring psychic-medium concepts with their pets rather than with other humans or even themselves. And they're more motivated to use the tools I teach with their pets rather than with themselves.

I believe this to be true because of the trust bond we form with our pets. We trust that they will not hurt us or intentionally let something bad happen. They protect us and love us unconditionally. And we can forgive their imperfections. We can believe that they have our best interest at heart and have our backs—and we have theirs! I've also learned that our animals act as "filters" for our physical and emotional pain. They empathically absorb our issues to help us. They also help us find our life purpose.

I work with a lot of people who have aging pets and those who are in the transitioning process. I cherish the opportunity to help people heal from the pets they've lost. Losing a pet, whether their pets don't come home or they have passed –it can be a traumatizing experience, and it's easy to get stuck in what I call "The Loop of Grief." I provide psychic-medium and end-of-life Doula support to help people move past their intense grief and find the joy in their lives that their pets so desperately want for them.

As a Medical Intuit, I believe it's helpful to provide different perspectives for people to consider while making decisions during recoveries and transitions.

Ladybug, and I hope that you find this information helpful. We appreciate your time exploring *Heal With Your Pet*.

Anna Breytenbach, Animal Communicator

Watch this heartfelt video about the incredible story of how Leopard Diabolo became known as Spirit. Anna is so talented, and I believe you will be inspired by watching her as I have been.

Use your camera to scan the QR code to explore the information

MEET MY PARTNER, LADYBUG

Ladybug🐞
Spirit Animal Guide & Reiki Master

Ladybug is my partner in the Spiritual work that I do. She has also become my service dog. *And she is great at both!* She entered my life when I rescued her in 2017 from a shelter. She was 18 months old, and I call her my "Georgia Peach!" Ladybug came to me in a dream the night before I picked her up. I planned to name her Lovebug, but in that dream, Ladybug clearly had other intentions and told me that she wanted to be called "Ladybug," not Lovebug. And she has clearly made her intentions known to me ever since!

Imagine the surprise on the caregivers' faces at the shelter when Ladybug completely ignored the name Kate (her shelter name) and instead immediately ran to me when I called her Ladybug! She only came to people who called her Ladybug from that point on! Her shelter caregivers asked me how she knew her name already – I told them about the dream that I had the night before when she told me her name was Ladybug. Yup, they felt she was going to the right home. *We had that kind of connection from day one!*

I adopted Ladybug on a Thursday, and the next day, I was teaching a Usui Holy Fire® III Reiki Master class. After a good bath, she came along with me. During the class, she approached each person and intuitively did healing work by lying on them, kissing them, and putting her paw over their heart. Amazingly, she paid special attention to the areas where my students were having symptoms. They all reported sensing her healing energy and felt better after that.

Within two hours of Ladybug being at my training site for the first time, she pulled a card from my tarot deck. I got this deck when I was 16 years old, and it was my first one. The interesting thing was that the card she picked was the one card in the deck that had no identification in the instruction book that came with the deck—the Arcus Arcanum Tarot.

It said nothing about it. So I decided to set the intention that it represented everything coming together in the right way and at the right time. When it came up in a reading, it represented dreams manifesting, and I took that to be a message from Spirit: that I was on one of my Life Purpose Healing Paths with Ladybug *(a High Vibrational Frequency)*.

Ladybug has guided me on a magical path of healing with animals. We collaborate during sessions and meditations, and to my amazement, we have even created a Spirit Animal Reiki Class together!

During my Pet Communication & Healing classes, Ladybug always gave gemstones to my students. In one of our classes, Ladybug brought a clearing stone to a student. She gently placed the stone on her chest and then got down. The woman's friend gasped in amazement and said that she had been concerned about her friend who had been diagnosed with pneumonia! She definitely took that stone home!

Ladybug helps me to feel confident, stay healthy, and heal from my past traumas. She'll come into the meditations that I do and help me provide healing and find solutions. She gives me a pet's perspective. She'll also do her own healing work on my animal clients and will alert me if that client needs something so we can collaborate.

Ladybug has guided and encouraged me to use my **Psychic-Medium** skills. She has also helped me in developing the Energetic Communication™ Language, which we will share with you in this book. Xoxo.

Picture taken on the first day of Reiki Master Class and the second day Ladybug had found her forever home!

1

INTRO-"DUCK"-TION

In this book, I'll share a new language that Ladybug and I learned together. At the end of this book is a *Glossary* with the definitions for my capitalized and bolded words that I suspect may be new to you. This new language is made up of three tools. There are many ways to clear, balance, and provide healing for our pets and keep them balanced and healed—and we'll share some in the chapters that follow. They can help us focus and clarify our intentions.

These three tools can foster better communication between animals and people. And from a psychic-energetic perspective, they can create a High Vibrational Healing Frequency.

WHY ANIMAL COMMUNICATION?

I've found that humans can be more comfortable exploring psychic-medium concepts with their pets than just on their own. I believe this is true because of the trust bond we form with many of our pets. We trust that they will not hurt us, and we can easily forgive their imperfections. Sometimes, we have a very strong bond and I call these **Karmic-Legacy Pets**. I believe that these are the very special pets that sometimes refer their humans to me... *LOL!*

Our capacity to experience love, joy, and gratitude naturally expands in the presence of animals. However, with our **Karmic-Legacy Pets**, it's amplified more than ten-fold. These emotions have **High Vibrational Frequency**. For me, this represents Spiritual energy.

I want to share how our animals act as "filters" for our physical, emotional, mental, energetic, and Spiritual pains—and especially about how our pets may empathically absorb our issues to help us. Our pets are what I call **The Perfect Empaths.**

It seems to me that the tools and skills we will learn to use with our pets here are exactly what we need to be successful in our **Human Experience.** Our pets act as mirrors for us, and they can help guide us to find our own **Life Purpose Healing Paths**—they can help us find our **Life Purpose.**

The three tools Ladybug and I will share with you make up an intuitive language—some might call it psychic language. It's a language we can use to communicate through the **Akashic Records**.

Here's the thing: I believe everyone already uses many of these tools and skills to communicate with their pets and each other. One of the three tools is made up of parts. We can think about these parts as the parts of speech, like nouns and verbs in the English Language. I call this the **Universal Language**.

I believe that the first language we naturally use as infants is this **Universal Language.** It's made up of images and emotions.

We "project" these images and emotions to our caregivers to get our needs met. The stronger the emotions, the clearer the image becomes, and the more our needs get met. Our pets also naturally use this language. But as we get older, we lose our confidence in using it.

This book offers many opportunities to find perspectives, tools, and skills that align with you and your pets. When I was a visiting nurse, I would tell my clients that I came to them with a *"Bouquet of Options... they can choose the ones they want and throw out the rest!"* Ladybug and I now offer that to you.

Pets do not want us to worry about them or to feel guilty about the decisions we are sometimes forced to make. They want us to be happy and feel loved unconditionally.

Our animals—pets and wild alike—need our help to clear the energy they absorb from the world and from us, balance their energy for healing to happen, and provide healing for the damage that has already been done. Ladybug and I will share ways to re-learn this language and the tools that can help that happen.

I call this language **Energetic Communication™.**

2

ENERGETIC COMMUNICATION™

THREE TOOLS FOR YOUR TOOLBOX

We are excited to share this foundational system that Ladybug and I created and use together every day. We call it **Energetic Communication™**. As I mentioned before, it consists of three tools that can be used to develop our communication and high vibrational healing skills with our pets. The tools are:

- Image-Emotion Sets™
- The Harmonic Energetic Set-Up™ & HESU™ Tool
- High Vibrational Healing Skills

Energetic Communication™ is an intuitive language, and it takes some time and commitment to learn. Just like any new language you decide to learn, it sometimes feels difficult, confusing, and can be misinterpreted. As you understand the tools and gain confidence in using them, they become quick, easy, and super effective! They become quick maintenance tools we can use during the busy times in our lives.

As you spend time using the three tools with your pets, notice any changes that arise. First, the specific changes we will like may not be the ones our pet will make. I encourage keeping a journal and watching for subtle changes; these can be things like sleeping in a different spot or playing with a different toy. Maybe they begin to eat, drink, or go to the bathroom differently. Perhaps they begin to look at you differently. They usually do become sleepy when we start building this foundation and using these tools. It's like how we feel after a healing session or learning new Spiritual skills. They are detoxing and adapting.

If we want to change undesirable behaviors or help our pets heal from an illness or emotional trauma, it will take time and fine-tuning of these skills. If you can commit to using these three tools consistently over the next three months, I believe these issues can improve. And I bet you will feel better too!

As we gain confidence in our ability to use the **Energetic Communication™** tools with our pets, we can begin to understand the messages they are sending to us too. The communication line gets clearer and becomes less static and confusing.

Ultimately, this system of communication and healing automatically helps us to heal along with our pets. As that happens, we develop a beautiful Spiritual Relationship that just grows stronger and never ends—even when our pets leave this world, we can always stay connected in a loving **Spiritual Relationship** with them. Our pets become our **Spirit Guides** from the other side.

As we build Spiritual Relationships with our pet-animal friends by setting the intention to help them heal, *we heal ourselves too, and we begin to heal the world together!*

While working with my clients, I've had the joy of witnessing the healing power of animals time and time again. We have a symbiotic relationship. By paying attention to the messages our animals are sending to us, we can gain insight into what to pay attention to in the world and in our own lives as well.

As we watch and listen to what's going on with our pets, we may discover that those things are issues that may be going on with us, friends, or family members as well.

Our rescue pets come to us with the **Legacy** of their previous lives. Sometimes, they come to us with behavioral issues and physical problems stemming from the emotional traumas of their past. I believe that these pets bring us messages about our life purpose and our undiscovered natural talents. We choose each other to be life partners at certain times for specific reasons in our lives.

I would like to use the **Analogy of The Rainforest** to describe the beautiful filtration and healing system we can create with our pets using Energetic Communication™. Just as the rainforest absorbs carbon dioxide and toxins from the world, our animals absorb pain, illness, and emotions from us. Simply put, the rainforest acts as a filter by collaborating with the rain and transmuting the toxins into oxygen.

Our pets are the rainforest, and we are the rain. Together, we can create the same kind of transmuting filtration system between us and the rainforest. The problem arises when we don't do our part. We must help them to clear, balance, and provide healing for them—because they cannot do it on their own. We are in a partnership, and when we collaborate amazing things can happen.

Ultimately, the goal is to create a maintenance plan using Energetic Communication™ with our pets. Most people find that working with these tools creates new confidence, better health, and peace in their lives and their pets'... *I know it has for us.*

We can use **Energetic Communication™** to connect and provide healing for the wild animals of the world too.

This leads us to the next chapter: You will find a quick and easy tool to clear, balance, and heal your pet. It can be used during busy times for maintenance so our pets can remain empathically healthy.

3

HARMONIC ENERGETIC SET-UP™ AND HESU™ TOOLS

The **Harmonic Energetic Set-Up™** starts as a two-step process that helps us to work with grounding, balancing, and healing energies. It can keep us and our pets in our own core energy, and it can create a **High Vibrational Field** that we can use to keep our pets clear of emphathically absorbing energy from us, others, and the world. I use it as a quick maintenance tool for my pets and myself, too.

Where did this tool come from? In 2015, it was downloaded to me by my **Spirit Guides** to help me manage empathic energy and share with others. *I've learned that when we absorb energy from others, our energy gets displaced.* The other person, animal, or situation empathically absorbs ours. This is because we live in space, and it can be confining. The energy we absorb gets "kicked out" because we have a limited amount of space in our body to hold other energies than our own. When this happens, we are not in our **Core Energy** anymore; we have others' energies too. It can become difficult for us to feel confident in making decisions, and our pets can react instead of responding.

My Spirit Guides downloaded this process to me through the guided meditations and Spiritual Mentoring that I do. They said we can't make good decisions, stay healthy, and find peace if we're not coming from our core, confident, and peaceful selves.

Have you ever been around someone who is very anxious or depressed, and you walk away feeling the same way? Or have you experienced when someone is angry at you, and you feel more anger toward them or less patient than you usually are?

These are examples of absorbing another's energy. It happens through the emotions they're feeling: empathic energy. Our animals absorb our energies all the time—like our emotions, illnesses, and pain. They do this to help us. It's one of the jobs they came into our lives to do.

Wild animals do this for the world. This is one reason we see dolphins and whales grounding themselves on land. They are telling us that something is up in the ocean nearby. And if we dig into the situation enough, they will give us messages about possible solutions with their actions.

Our animals "shoulder" our imperfections until we can heal them ourselves. It's a karmic agreement we made before our current lifetime together—and nothing to feel guilty about. In fact, when we can feel grateful for their help, and in listening to their messages - we heal, they heal, and the world heals. Win, win, and win.

I have had multiple abdominal problems and surgeries, and one day, when I was on the ground in pain, my dog Sadie helped me. I was on the ground on all fours—she rubbed against me, then walked underneath me, rubbing against my belly—and my abdominal pain was gone! She was an amazing Healer!

I saw a home video on the Today Show that is a great example of how our pets take on our pain and mirror our behavior. This unfortunate person had injured his right foot or ankle. He had a cast on, and the video showed him coming down the hall using crutches, carefully avoiding any pressure on his injured right foot. Following right behind him was his cat—it too, was limping along with its right paw up. It was empathetic to its human's condition and doing its best to help. The cat had not been injured. Bless that cat!

The HESU Set-Up™ and the HESU™ Tool work great for our pets. In fact, since they don't have preconceived notions about "healing tools" and whether they work or not... and wonder if it's all in their heads (like we do) —*they experience the effects faster.* You may notice them responding by changing positions, changing certain behaviors, or looking at you with a surprised look on their face. The more we use this tool with them, the healthier they become, *and so can we!*

Step One: The Harmonic Energetic Set-Up™

1. Ground Energy—*Lower arms toward the ground.*
2. Connect them to their **Higher Self** and **Spirit Animal**—*Raise hands toward the sky.*
3. Two filters form and surround your pet, forming an egg shape—*Bring your hands down around them and connect with their grounding cord.*
   - A **Moon Light Filter** energizes their **Auric Field** and magnetizes health to them.
   - The **Holy Fire Violet Flame** filter does not burn—it transmutes the empathic energy flowing through the filter in both directions.

Step Two: The HESU™ Tool

1. Clear Their Energy
2. Balance Their Energy
3. Heal Their Energy

This process returns our pet's foreign energy back to where it came from and recalls their own energy back to them. *And it's always for the highest good of all.* Now they are in their healthy core self-energy.

This is the foundation, and there are lots of great ways to build on it.

USING THE HESU™ TOOL WITH YOUR PET

Step One: Harmonic Energetic Set-Up™:

1. Rub your hands together until you feel the warmth. If you know **Reiki**, place the symbols in your palms. Point your palms toward your pet and lower them toward the ground, then visualize their energy forming a grounding cord, like the roots of a tree, extending down to and connecting with **Mother Earth's Lava Core.**

2. Slowly raise your hands and visualize the lava flowing back up through their **Grounding Cord.** It flows up and into their bodies, filling them with healing plasma energy that contains the nutrition and hydration their body needs. It also opens, clears, balances, and sets their **Chakra System** just right for them.

3. Continue to raise your hands toward the heavens and ask the plasma to connect with your pet's **Spirit Animal Guides.**

4. Bring your arms and hands down around them and visualize two filters forming around them to connect again with Mother Earth's Lava Core and their **Grounding Cord.** The filters form a vacuum tube of healthy energy that keeps them in their core energy.

5. The two filters form and surround them:
   • **The Moon Light Filter**
   • **The Holy Fire Violet Flame Filter**

Your pet is now set up with the foundation for the HESU™ Tool. So, let's use the tool!

Step Two: Use The HESU™ Tool:

1. Bring your hands toward the middle of your pet.
2. Wiggle your toes and say:
   - **I Clear** (their name) **Energy:**
     Flick your fingers while moving your hands outward in opposite directions. This releases the empathic energy they have absorbed back to where it belongs.
   - **I Balance** (their name) **Energy:**
     Move your arms up and down, focusing on creating a flow of **Plasma Energy** moving within the filter system, from their **Spirit Animal Guides** to Mother Earth and back.
   - **I ask that** (their name) **Energy be Healed**:
     Move your hands as if you were holding the outside of their filters and ask that their energy be healed by their **Spirit Animal Guides**. This returns their energy.

All their energy is cleared, balanced, and healed as it travels through the filters. It is transmuted to create high vibrational healing energy for the highest good of all!

When we absorb each other's energy, we become entwined with one another. When this happens, neither we nor our pets respond from our authentic selves and healthy core energy. Instead, we react to a mixture of our and others' energies. When we can keep our pets' energy clear and balanced, they naturally heal, and we heal along with them.

HESU™ River of Possibilities Tool is used to do focused clearing, balancing, and healing between us and our pets. Our empathic energy returns to us, and theirs returns to them. It's a very important step in creating a healthy filtration system between humans and their pets, as I spoke of it earlier. This tool allows the **Universal Life Force Energy** to flow between and around us.

We can set the intention that this energy becomes a continuous river that flows around our filters and creates space between us and our pets. This is how we can stay grounded in our healthy core self-energy and not be entwined with each other. When we create space between us and our pets, we are both able to communicate more clearly and become healthier.

Our pets continuously absorb toxic energy from us to help us be the best we can be. When we give their energy back to them and call our energy back to us using this tool, the energy flows through both our filter systems. It transmutes into healthy, high vibrational energy as it returns. Space needs to be created between us for this to happen; otherwise, our energies will remain empathically entwined. This creates a healthy filtration system, like the rainforest analogy I used earlier.

If we do this regularly as healthy maintenance work for our pets, we can help them stay healthy, and we feel better, too.

Instructions:

1. Set you and your pet up with the HESU™ Tool.
2. Set an intention and visualize a river flowing between and around you both. This is the **River of Possibilities** (Universal Life Force Energy)
3. Allow it to widen and shrink.

SAY:

1. I call the energy that you absorbed from me back to me.
2. I give the energy I absorbed from you back to you.
3. All the entwined empathic energy releases and returns transmuted into the highest good for you and your pet.

I call it **The River of Possibilities** because you just never know what surprises Spirit will drop in! When we're empathically entwined, we leave no room for the magic that can happen and opportunities to drop into our lives.

Again, our pets are helping us heal, gain clarity, set boundaries, and stay in our own core energy. As we practice with them and see the results, we can confidently use this in our own lives, too. Spirit needs space to communicate with us, and so do our pets. They, too, speak the same language—it's universal!

This is the filter system that I spoke of earlier. Our pets replace our toxic energy with their healing energy.

The more we use the **HESU™ Tool** and **The River of Possibilities Tool**, the healthier we both become. Our pets, like the rainforest, absorb our toxic energy, and we can cleanse, balance, and provide healing for us both by calling it back to us and returning their energy through the filtration system we have created.

We are the rain. Our intentions are necessary to clear, balance, and heal their energies. We must choose to be the rain. When we work with this tool and create a maintenance schedule, we can create a constant cycle of healing between us and our pets.

That is one of the most important jobs that our pets came into our lives to do for us. By helping us stay in our core energy with lots of space for new and exciting things, Spirit can drop opportunities into our world.

Why can't our pets do this themselves? As I mentioned before, they do not perceive time the way we do. This is self-care, and it takes time to make the decision and choose to do it. Even when we decide to do self-care now, it still takes a second or two to do it.

It is possible to teach our pets to stay in their **Harmonic Energetic Set-Up™** for periods of time, like when they go to the veterinarian or daycare. They need us to provide structure maintenance to keep themselves clear of empathic energy. Using the **HESU™ Tools** makes it quick and easy to continue doing.

Now you know the **Harmonic Energetic Set-Up™** and some of the **HESU™ Tools** that Spirit downloaded to me. As you use the tools, they become a quick and easy way to keep our pets happy, healthy, and safe. They are meant to be used as a maintenance tools moving forward.

The **HESU™ Tool** has worked amazingly well for myself, my clients, and for all the animals I have worked with in the wild and at zoos. I hope you find it as helpful as it has been for all of us!

Harmonic Energetic Set-Up™ Program

Experience some more detailed animations, videos, and pictures of the HESU™ in action! You can imagine replacing the human in the animations with your pet.

Use your camera to scan the QR code to explore the information. Enjoy!

Let's move on to the next tool in **Energetic Communication™: Image-Emotion Sets™.**

4

THE UNIVERSAL LANGUAGE

IMAGE-EMOTION SETS™

There is a **Universal Language**, and I believe we're all born knowing how to speak it. It's made up of images that we visualize in our minds and the emotions that accompany them.

So, the first step in developing Energetic Communication™ is building our "parts of speech"—I call them **Image-Emotion Sets™**.

We all used them when we were infants and children. It was the only way we could communicate to get our needs met before we learned our family's verbal and written language. As we grew up and learned verbal and written language, our ability to visualize took the back seat, and many of us learned that emotions were "bad" unless they were very controlled. As a result, our ability to use the universal language that we were born with diminished—and, for some, disappeared.

Those of us who still use universal language are called sensitive, creative, artists, problem solvers, empaths, intuitive, psychics, mediums, insightful, and mentally ill, among other names.

Social media has become a great place to find examples of the universal language at work. Look for a video of a child who wants something, and their pet is with them. The pet just understands; no words are needed. Their pet may be giving snuggles, opening doors, or protecting them from danger. They're responding to what the child is imagining and feeling—it's telepathy, and we can all do it. It's poetic to watch children with their pets. This is the **Universal Language of Image-Emotion Sets™** in action, and it's a powerful skill that can be re-learned. I will guide you as you continue in this book.

Let me ask you: Have you ever just "known" what your child or pet wanted? Does your pet know when you are coming home? Have you ever thought about someone, and then they call you, or vice versa? Those are examples of the **Universal Language** at work.

How cool is it to watch entertainers with their animals? Watch AGT's 2023 winner, Adrian Stoica and Hurricane, win the season 18 finale. There were no verbal words spoken between them. Body language, yes; however, there is much more to it than just the physical. I have heard other performers report that their pets just do what they are thinking. That's the universal language, and we can all "speak" it. Not all of us will wind up being performers on AGT—because that is not one of our **Life Purpose Paths.**

This language works in both directions. As we re-learn these skills, our pets communicate back to us in the same way. Have you ever just gotten an image in your mind of giving your pet a treat, feeding them, or giving them a bathroom break? And then they are sitting at the cookie jar, bowl, or door? Do you ever feel like their eyes are piercing your soul? They are sending **Image-Emotion Sets™** to us.

These are all examples of **Image-Emotion Sets™.** You have an image or thought, along with an emotion, and it gets amplified and broadcast to your pet and other people.

I believe that we have all been communicating intuitively with our pets this way all along. The key is being conscious of this type of communication, slowing it down, and actively using it. **Image-Emotion Sets™** slow our thoughts down and amplify the message with our emotions so our pets can understand us better.

Some people are more successful at this than others and can send or receive **Image-Emotion Sets™** quite easily. For some, it's more difficult. The more disconnected one is with one's ability to visualize, the more difficult it will be to re-learn and re-connect the neural networks that support the universal language. Sometimes, our images and emotions don't match up, which can be confusing to both us and our pets.

If you believe you cannot visualize, no worries; you can reawaken that part of your brain. It just has not been used in a while. And just like building muscle, rebuilding the neural connections at first may be sore and uncomfortable. Some people develop actual headaches and can have physical sensations as they re-connect and use this language skill. That is because new neural pathways and ridges are literally growing in the brain and body. It can be uncomfortable.

* * * * *

This is what I have learned about how to focus and build confidence in our ability to use the **Universal Language**.

Each **Image-Emotion Set™** is a part of the Universal Language . Let's create your first **Image-Emotion Set™.**

Ladybug's Happy, Peaceful, & Safe Picture

Start with a picture.

1. Find a picture of your pet where they are snuggled up and sleeping. They look like they feel happy, peaceful, and safe.
2. How does this picture make you feel?
3. Spend 30 seconds looking at the picture and feeling the emotions that this image brings up for you, like peace, joy, gratitude, etc. These are considered high vibrational emotions.

Over the next few days, look at this picture and deeply feel those emotions. Each time you do so that part of speech grows stronger and clearer for your pet to "hear."

The next step is to visualize that picture and feel those emotions at the same time. Start doing this as much as possible with this image. Do it when you are around your pet and when you are not—the more you do it, the easier it gets and the stronger the message gets. You are telling your pet that their alpha wants them to feel happy, peaceful, and safe!

Congratulations—you have created your first Image-Emotion Set™. Over the next week, notice how your pet responds to you and other things in its environment.

- How do they act and respond when you are using that **Image-Emotion Set™**?
- Are there any changes in their behaviors?
- Are they different around other people or animals?

Don't worry if you don't notice any changes; it takes time, and we can easily miss some subtle changes to begin with. It's helpful to keep a pet communication journal so you can look back and see things you missed at the time. Remember when I said, just like learning any new human language, it's sometimes difficult, confusing, and misinterpreted? This is when that happens. You're just starting to develop your intuitive communication skills with your pet. They may become confused at first. This can easily happen with rescue pets and animals who have suffered emotional, genetic, and or physical traumas. Just keep going. If they respond in any way, it's working and will become easier and clearer.

Let me suggest another **Image-Emotion Set™** to create so you can create a strong foundation.

- Find a picture of your pet looking happy, confident, and healthy.
- How does this picture make you feel?
- Spend 30 seconds looking at the picture and feeling the emotions that this image brings up for you, like happiness, joy, gratitude, etc. These are considered high vibrational emotions.

Ladybug's Happy, Confident, & Healthy Picture

You will soon be able to create more and more **Image-Emotion Sets™** just by visualizing a snapshot image of what you want to communicate combined with the high vibration emotions associated with it. As our neural network reconnects to our "infant" brain, we can become fluent in the universal language.

When we create more and more **Image-Emotion Sets™**, they will string together into "sentences" that then become a "non-spoken" intuitive language. It will become easier to create and use new **Image-Emotion Sets™**. The more we create and use, the faster they will start to string together and become an intuitive communication—a **Universal Language**. When that happens, we can communicate automatically and instinctively with each other before even putting words to our thoughts. Now, we are speaking our pet's language!

It's important to understand how our pets perceive our thoughts and emotions. Animals, in general, pay attention to the strongest emotions they feel from us. They base their mindful actions on the most intense vibrational frequency they feel in the moment. I'll discuss vibrational frequencies more in Chapter Nine. Below are some examples of what my clients, both pets and humans, have told me. Do any of these feel familiar?

Example 1

You're on your way home and can't wait to see your pets. You imagine their loving faces, and you feel happy and excited to see them. You spend time visualizing these images and feeling these emotions with gratitude.

You clearly communicate to them that you're on your way home and everything is okay with their world. They respond by being at the door or looking out the window ten minutes before you arrive home. That's because you communicated to your pet with **Image-Emotion Sets™** that you were on your way home.

Image - Walking in and seeing their loving face.

Emotions - Happiness, excitement, and gratitude.

Example 2a

Your pet has separation anxiety and often acts out. When you leave, you're thinking about what you can do to stop them from feeling scared and acting out. You're worried about them. Maybe you're feeling guilty, sad, frustrated, or ashamed you don't know what to do.

Your pet's perspective:

My human is concerned, so there must be something wrong. I need to protect something. Is my human in danger, or am I? They are really worried, fearful, and scared (low vibration emotions). I better do something!

Image - What they do when they act out.

Emotions - Fear, anger, shame, guilt, sadness.

Example 2b

Now, you are coming home to your pet with separation anxiety. You start having anxiety about coming home. Perhaps you feel fearful about what your pet may have done while you were away. Maybe you feel guilty for leaving them. Are you imagining things they have done in the past when you were gone, like ripping up the couch, going through the trash, or destroying their crate? What are you thinking, and what are the most intense emotions you are feeling? And how much time did you spend thinking about those images and feeling those emotions?

Your pet's perspective:

My human is coming home, and they are not happy, feeling balanced, or feeling safe! I must have done something wrong. I see they want me to fluff up the couch, empty the trash, or get out of my crate because it's not safe.

Image - What they do when they act out.

Emotions - Anxiety, fear, anger, shame, guilt, sadness.

In all these examples, you are visualizing your pet doing exactly what you don't want them to do.

Our pets want to please us, which is why they jump to attention, and if they have not already done what you are telling them to do with your **Image-Emotion Sets™**, they will make sure they get it done before you get home. Or they may surprise you with something new, they could do exactly what you didn't want them to do depending on the images and emotions you have spent the most time on. See how the messages can be confusing to them? The lines of communication are crossed. There is hope!

Low Vibrational Emotions like anxiety, fear, anger, shame, guilt, sadness, and hopelessness will result in a fight-or-flight reaction from our pets rather than the response we hope for. They don't decipher our emotions as good or bad, positive or negative, right or wrong, or what we do or do not want. Animals just **React** to our low vibration emotions and **Respond** to our high vibrational emotions. The emotions that are the most intense and we feel for the longest time win, either good or bad, high or low. So, then they will try to figure out what image in our minds goes with the emotion we are feeling and then react or respond.

This may sound like I am blaming humans for all their pets' problems. That is just our guilt talking. This is one of our pets' jobs, and they are happy to help us. It is a more productive perspective to consider the things our pets are doing right. That's where we focus on the high vibrational emotions and can feel confident in our abilities.

I see the problems that our pets have as roadblocks to slow us down so we can learn to take care of ourselves by taking care of them. They teach us with their behaviors. They can guide us to our own happiness and teach us the tools to use for ourselves. Ultimately, the outcome can be that we heal them, which heals us, and then we heal the world together.

* * * * *

One of my pet clients thought their human wanted them to make dinner every night. The pet was ok with that and loved their job. They went through the trash and counter-surfed to find scraps to make dinner when they could. Sometimes, their humans put them somewhere that they could not get to the kitchen. The pet told me they thought they were not doing it right, and that's why their humans were not "happy" with dinner. They desperately needed to understand what their humans wanted so they could do it right.

During our session together, I found out that one of the behaviors their humans wanted them to stop was tearing up the garbage and counter-surfing!

When the human would come home, their pet would have had everything torn up in piles all over the floor. Their human was clearly upset with the mess!

Their pet reacted by shrinking away from them because the emotions did not feel comforting, not because they understood they were being bad.

Of course, the human was hoping their pet would understand their deep displeasure at their behavior and stop tearing up the garbage and counter surfing. Their pet was hoping to get it right, and based on their human's strongest emotion and images, they clearly were not.

PET'S PERSPECTIVE:

Ok, my human is sending **Image-Emotions Sets™** of me making dinner. Where can I get the food from? A trash can and counter are my best bet. I will put them in piles so we can eat together, and they can choose what they want.

It puts a different spin on things, doesn't it? I asked the client's human to send me a picture of the floor. We all laughed as we saw that their pet had torn the paper up to look like bones and crafted a nice mix of options in each pile of garbage on the floor for their human to choose from. Let's have dinner together!

So, what do you think about during your day? What default emotions do you feel? Not just about your pet but also about other things. What percent of your thoughts are of anxiety, fear, anger, worry, and guilt (low vibration emotions) vs. peace, love, joy, and gratitude (high vibration emotions)? Maybe you can expand your range of higher-vibration emotions with your pet's help.

The first few times our pets reacted in undesirable ways were about doing what they thought we wanted, based on their own survival instincts. After that, it became a learned behavior and pattern with neural pathways formed. This is when it becomes more difficult to change their behavior because they now believe that this is the right thing to do, and they have become "programmed" to do it. We continue to reinforce their behaviors or correct them with the **Image-Emotion Sets™** we consciously use. So, every time we react with low vibration emotions and images of what we don't want, we confirm it.

This is when it can turn into a **Post Traumatic Stress Disorder (PTSD) Triggers.** Their survival instinct becomes activated with low vibrational emotions and images, and they react to them instead of responding as we would like them to. We'll discuss more about how to handle these reactions in Chapter Seven, Neurological Deficits and PTSD Trauma.

Remember, it's the images or visualizations that we spend the longest time thinking about that instruct them on what to do based on the most intense emotion we feel.

Rescue pets can have many PTSD triggers from their past experiences, and we usually do not know what happened to them before we adopted them. It can be like a puzzle to figure it out. This is a good time to enlist a **Pet Psychic-Medium** to gain clarity and find out!

Like PTSD triggers in humans, the reactions our pets have are typically over-reactional and defensive. This is because their fight-or-flight nervous system is activated. Suddenly, they think they're going to die, and they must defend themselves and the ones they love. They react in the best way they can.

Along with the **Energetic Communication™ Tools** this book outlines, you will need to incorporate more healing techniques. You can consider holistic veterinarians, behavioral training, reiki and gemstones, flower essences, and neural restructuring, to name a few. I'll dive into all of this more in the chapters to follow.

But there is hope—I've seen my clients break this cycle with **High Vibrational Image-Emotion Sets™** and the healing techniques I teach. Using the higher-vibration emotions of love, compassion, praise, joy, and gratefulness rather than lower-vibration emotions can make all the difference.

I love Cesar Milan and his television series "*Better Humans, Better Dogs.*" This does not only apply to dogs but to all pets. Our pets look to their humans for guidance, and Cesar is a master of the compassionate, supportive, and effective techniques he uses—they don't call him The Dog Whisperer for nothing! Watch his series and add the tools you learn there with mine. I believe you'll have a winning combination.

* * * * *

BUILD YOUR IMAGE-EMOTION SET™ MUSCLE WITH THIS EXERCISE.

There are three images on the next pages. Look at one image at a time for 30 seconds or more before moving to the next one. Notice the emotion that the image brings up. Spend time looking at one image and feeling the emotion before moving on to the next image:

- What do you think?
- What did you feel?
- What is the image in your mind right now?
- Any other observations?

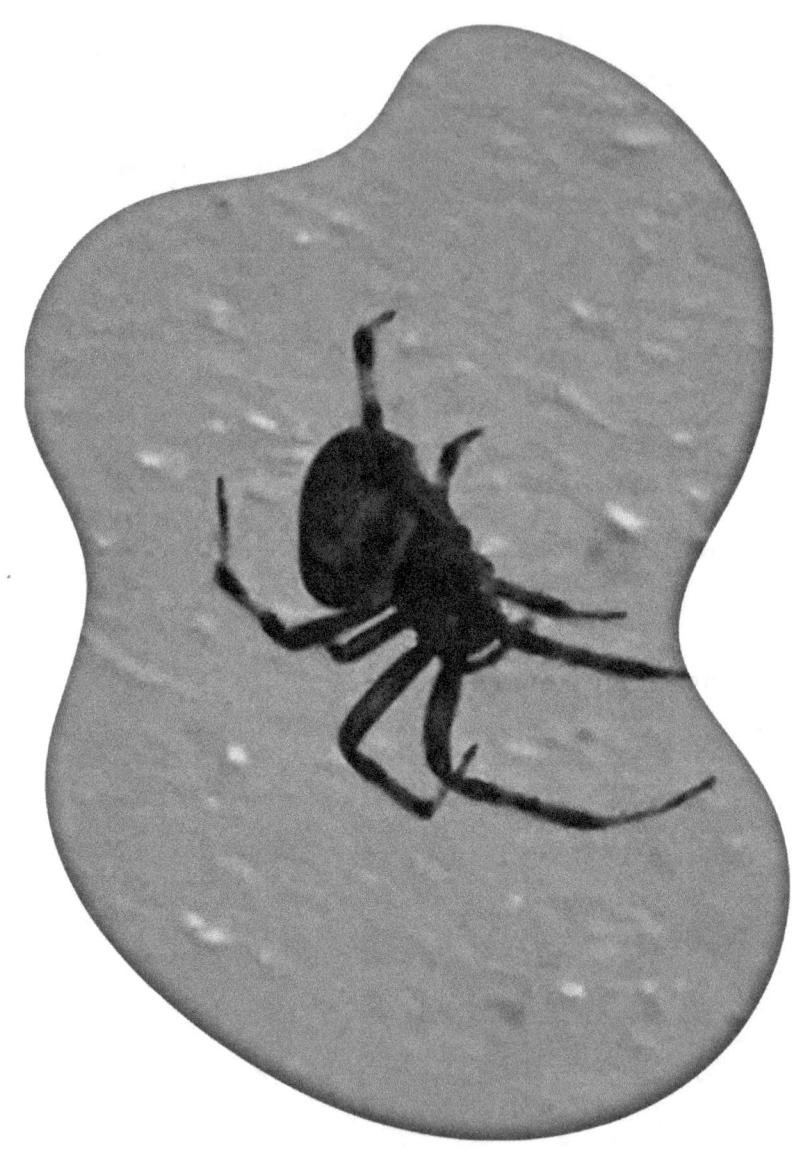

- What did you think?
- What do you feel?
- What is the image in your mind right now?
- Any other observations?

- What did you think?
- What do you feel?
- What is the image in your mind right now?
- What do you think the picture is?

Consider these questions too:

- Which image brought the strongest emotion?
- What was the emotion?
- How many different emotions did you feel?
- How quickly were you able to change your emotions from one image to the next?
- What image and emotions are sticking with you right now?

The last question usually indicates a person's go-to emotions in life. This is the emotion our pet most often feels from us. Ask yourself: how often do you have those same emotions during your day, at work, at play, and during self-care?

What did you think about the last image? Were you confused? Did you know what it was? The bats at the Stone Zoo in Stoneham, MA, told me that this confusion is how animals perceive most humans. Every bat represents an image in a human's mind. When you watch a group of bats, you'll notice that some are calm, some are fighting, and some are affectionate, and they are all communicating with each other.

What draws your attention first? Safety is usually our first impulse, so most likely, it would be the ones that are fighting and are chaotic. That is sometimes what our pets are "seeing and feeling" from us. They're trying to figure out what we want them to do. They are paying attention to the most intense emotion and reacting or responding to it the best way they can.

They will watch our body posture and then listen to what we are verbalizing to them. What we say matters the least to our pets. Our verbal language is confusing to them—and I must admit it is to me as well—LOL.

Like those bats, our thoughts and emotions change all the time. It's hard for our pets to figure out what image goes with what emotion. Now add these perspectives to the mix: "Is that my human talking to me or someone else? Does my human need my help? Do I need help?" Imagine their confusion. *Yep, bless their cotton socks!*

If you're like me, your emotions and thoughts do not always line up. I can get stuck in low vibration emotions like fear of judgment, anger, guilt, worry, anxiety, and sometimes hopelessness. These are my go-to **low vibration emotions**.

Emotions are considered energy, and each one has a different vibrational frequency (Hz). Did you know that our body functions around 68 Hz? And we can improve our health and our pets' health with the emotion of gratitude, which is 900-1000 Hz.

The chart on this page gives you an idea of how different illnesses can affect the energetic frequencies in our bodies. Notice that having a positive thought can raise the energetic frequency in our physical bodies by +10 Hz. Wait till you see how **high vibrational emotions** can affect our energetic frequencies. It goes to reason that staying in high vibrational emotions can help heal the physical body, just as the lower ones hurt it.

ENERGETIC FREQUENCIES	
FREQUENCY	**RESULT**
62-68 Hz	Healthy body
55 Hz	Candida symptoms
42 Hz or less	Cancer
-12 Hz	Negative thoughts
+10 Hz	Positive thoughts

Source: Dr. Gary Young

Our positive emotions have a higher energetic frequency, and they flow and change throughout our day like other waves do (vibrate). *This is why the* **Image-Emotions Sets™** *work so well!* We can use our images to invoke high vibration emotions to change the frequency we are communicating and change our pets' reactions to healthy responses. And they'll always respond to the higher vibrational emotions over the low vibrational emotions.

Image-Emotion Set™ Webinar

Watch a 12-minute Webinar explaining more about Image-Emotion Sets™.

Use your camera to scan the QR code to explore the information

Check out this chart. It is interesting to see the different vibrational frequencies of our emotions.

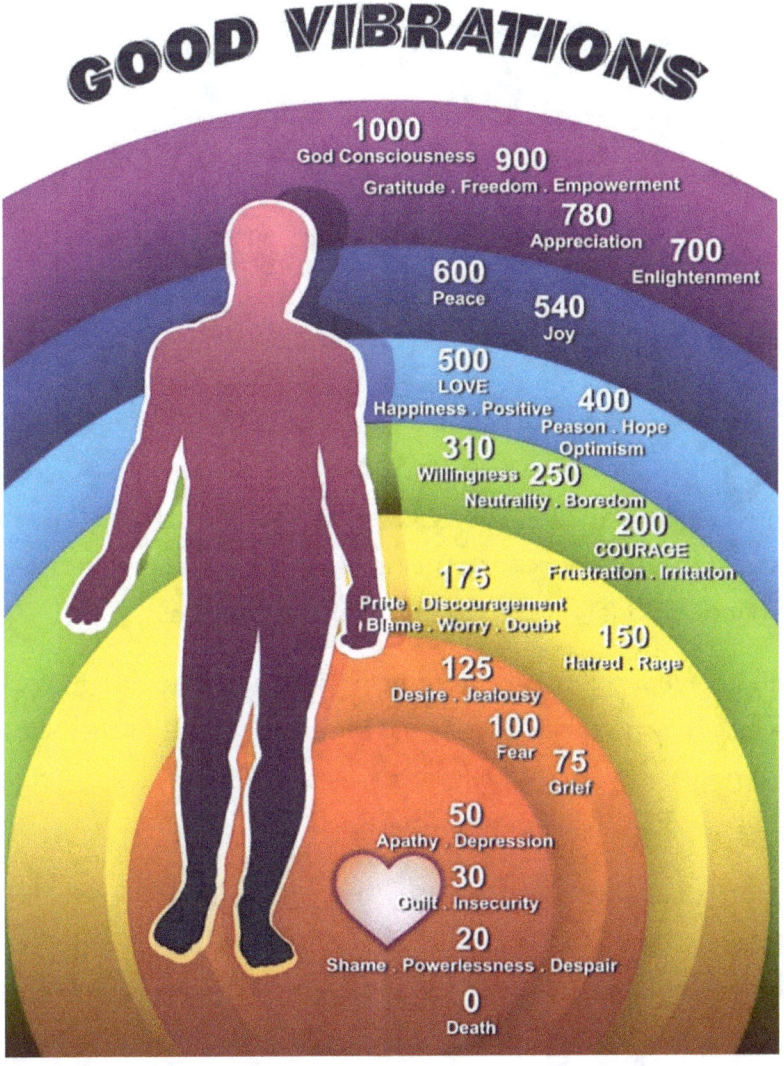

5

GOALS, JOBS, & MESSAGES

Now, let's explore some of the goals, jobs, and messages our pets have for us. They fill important roles in our lives with their love, and they give us opportunities for growth and greater spiritual connection. They expand our capacity to receive and give unconditional love, acceptance, and forgiveness.

Goals are what our pets want to help us to learn and heal from. **Jobs** are what they do for us to help us. **Messages** are what they show us about ourselves with the behaviors they are mirroring back. They can help us become aware of where we are wounded.

Animals take pride in their jobs. If they don't feel confident in performing their jobs, emotional and behavioral issues can arise. An example is when they try to be alpha when they're more naturally submissive. We can help them become more confident by being grateful and acknowledging them for doing their job well.

How do you feel when you are doing something you are not cut out for? Have you ever had a job where you felt you were over your head? Did you feel confident in that job? We can change our pets' behaviors by redirecting them to stay neutral to their undesirable behaviors and praise their natural behaviors.

We can identify their natural job by watching what they do. When they seem confident and happy about what they are doing, that is a natural and healthy job for them. Ask yourself, if your pet were in their wild environment, what do you think their job would be? How would they act in comparison with others of their species? Once you identify it, provide them opportunities to do it and praise them like crazy!

As their leaders, we can provide grateful and joyous feedback on their healthy behaviors. When we guide them to do the jobs they're meant to do, their behaviors change, and we are all much happier. Our pets become more confident. When we support healthy behaviors with high vibration emotions and ignore the "bad" behaviors, the undesirable behaviors can change faster.

It takes time, and this can be a tough switch for us humans. I call it "Switching our Flip"—LOL. I recommend using the go-to **Image-Emotion™ Set** we created earlier to change the vibrational frequency of the emotional situation.

Example:

Ladybug's natural jobs would be as a shaman and scout for the pack. She would be one of alpha mama's helpers. She would make sure the perimeter around the pups was safe and that they had what they needed while mama was away.

I had to understand that I needed to give her "sniff time" along with "no-sniffing time" on our walks. I needed to be in charge and instruct her. That was not the case at first. I would become irritated on walks when she would constantly keep peeing and sniffing, peeing and sniffing ... This was her telling me that she was nervous about her surroundings and needed to protect us both by sniffing for danger and scent marking everywhere.

One of her natural jobs was to scout small areas with a specific purpose: to protect the pups. I was not directing her where to do this, so she overreacted to her job and did it everywhere. I was the pup and not the alpha. I also realized that I was really the one who felt nervous about my surroundings. Throughout the pandemic, I became borderline agoraphobic (fearful of leaving my home). Ladybug was absorbing my low vibration emotions of fear, anxiety, and distrust of the outside environment and mirroring them back to me.

When I realized this, I started directing her where to scout and when to pee. It took a bit, and it takes continued maintenance. When she falls back into her "old behaviors," I know I'm falling back into mine. I check how I am showing up for myself, and if needed, I do some maintenance. Ladybug is still training me... *hahaha!*

As we have worked on this issue, I created three **Image-Emotion Sets™**:

1. Ladybug is engaging in her natural and healthy scouting behavior, and I am grateful and proud of her.
2. Ladybug is walking next to me on a loose leash, and we are feeling peaceful, confident, and curious about our surroundings.

3. Ladybug is confident and happy when other dogs or humans are approaching. We feel grateful, happy, secure, and safe.

Body posture is an effective addition to **Image-Emotions Sets™**. I relax my shoulders, look ahead, and feel my feet connecting with Mother Earth. As I mentioned before, Cesar Milan, The Dog Whisperer, demonstrates this very well. He has helped me become more confident through my dogs, past and present. I highly recommend combining our tools.

For other pet species, I recommend using the same tools we are teaching and seeing an image of your pet instead. You can also search some YouTube videos to find a Behaviorist who specializes in your pet species. There are a bunch of talented animal trainers, healers, and communicators. It's important to find the ones who align with our jobs, goals, and messages for our pets.

* * * * *

Throughout the years, animals have talked with me about their jobs, messages, and needs. Here are some general examples of what they've told me:

What our animals do for us:

Birds: They make us laugh, cry, angry, and feel healthy. They help us feel and love our own uniqueness and sensualities.

Cats: They give us spiritual awareness and physical healing, protect us and our living environment from Spiritual entities, and remind us to set boundaries. They are Shamans and Angels at the same time.

Dogs: They are the specialists providing support, protection, physical healing, compassion, and unconditional love. In English, "dog," spelled backward, is "God." I know this because I am dyslexic, and it was the first word that made sense to me the first time I read it out loud.

I read right to left... *hahaha!*

Horses: They connect our physical and emotional minds to heal deep wounds, provide friendship and are our companions. They help us rewire our neural networks and give us structure.

Pigs: They encourage us to be adventurous and creative in our actions. They teach us to be protective of our intentions for our family and friends.

Snakes: They are teachers of peace and encourage us to shed our struggles, pain, and fears. They remind us to stay energetically grounded to Mother Earth, to slow down, and to use caution when making big decisions. Consider the consequences first, and don't react solely to emotions (*i.e., hiss before you strike!*).

Spiders: They remind us to stop and consider boundaries, options, and different perspectives. What other viewpoints, solutions, and opportunities are being offered, no matter how small? With eight legs, eight eyes, and an amazing ability to catch themselves when they fall, they mirror these abilities for us. Look at a situation in a different way and be curious. Ask another person for their perspective on your situation. Stop and feel the vibrational frequency of the emotions around you... like a web.

Wild Animals: They deliver specific messages about the health of our planet and give warnings of environmental catastrophes. They give us messages about solutions when we listen. They are also our **Spirit Animal Specialists.** For example, when an animal crosses our path and we take notice, they typically have a message for us. The animals I have communicated with are happy to guide you with their messages too, if you ask. Sometimes, I google the names of the animals I see and read the first message that comes up.

Example: try "bird spirit animal"

What our animals need from us:

Birds: Need Friends

Cats: Need Grounding

Dogs: Need Jobs

Horses: Need Connection

Pigs: Need Adventures

Snakes: Need Peace

Spiders: Need Options

Wild Animals: Need us to listen.

Another important perspective to consider is that animals are the perfect empaths. And pets are empathically connected to their humans. They absorb energy, but they are not able to clear it on their own. We can choose to do self-care for ourselves—animals appreciate self-care too.

When we choose to do something, it takes time. Even if we decided to do it now, it still takes a second to make that decision. Animals do not experience time as we do, so they cannot "choose" to clear, balance, and heal themselves. They cannot decide to do self-care like we can.

In the next chapter, let's explore how we can use Energetic Communication™ when managing Behavioral Concerns.

6

BEHAVIORAL CONCERNS

I work with a lot of clients who are having sudden or ongoing behavioral problems with their pets. Things like going to the bathroom in the house, separation anxiety, or aggression, to name a few. It's important to seek a medical consultation with a veterinarian immediately.

There may be an underlying health issue that a pet is trying to communicate with their change in behavior. If there is a health problem, hopefully, it can be treated and quickly resolved along with the behavioral concern as well.

For example, Ladybug will start to pee in the house, in my chair, and in bed when she's trying to let me know she does not feel well and needs to see Dr. Downey, her veterinarian and bestie. She usually has a urinary tract infection, and when treated, her undesirable behavior stops immediately.

Once health issues are ruled out, then we can work on other reasons and solutions for the behavioral concerns.

When our pets don't feel confident doing the job they were naturally meant to do, they assume a role of defense or retreat. This is when we can see undesirable behavioral changes. They can be temporary or ongoing and are unhealthy behaviors. Sometimes, they become dangerous for us or others.

Cesar Milan, "The Dog Whisperer," explains these as red-light behaviors, meaning they need to be addressed ASAP. Biting, threatening, posturing, or attacking other animals and people are the big ones, especially if they draw blood. A consultation with a professional trainer, veterinarian, and, of course, a pet psychic-medium are great places to start. Seek help from many sources when a red-light behavior is present.

Cesar Millan – The Dog Wisper
Watch this short YouTube video that introduces Cesar's philosophy on dogs that are reactive and have separation anxiety.

Use your camera to scan the QR code to explore the information

I also recommend working with a behaviorist who specializes in your pet's species. Adding the tools and meditations in this book can help speed up the recovery process and allow you and your pet to gain or regain confidence and balance.

For example, as I previously mentioned, Ladybug's natural job in the pack would have been to be a scout, specifically for the pups. She would not be responsible for scouting while the pack was on the move, only when the pack would be stationary. That would be her Alpha's job.

Ladybug's unhealthy behavior of constantly sniffing and marking on our walks became a behavioral concern. The more frustrated I got, the worse her behavior became. When I changed my behavior, hers changed too. I always tell her what a good job she's doing when I instruct her where to scout. She is such a good scout!

Another issue we were having was timely pooping, especially in new places. She would growl and constantly look around. It took her forever to find a spot; OMG, I became so frustrated, which made things even worse.

She knew I was upset and worried. She thought there was really something wrong if I was that upset (**low vibrational emotions**). It stressed her out and made her insecure instead of confident. She was reacting by not pooping instead of finding a place and knowing I had her back. There were a few messages she was communicating to me through her behaviors.

First, she did not trust the space because if her own alpha was not calm and trusting of it, why should she be?

Second, she was giving me messages about my own insecurities and the behaviors that were causing me problems in my life. For instance, I was very insecure about using public bathrooms and did not feel confident and safe in many social settings. Besides the trauma from my past that I am still working on, I became agoraphobic (fearful of leaving my home) during the pandemic of 2020.

Ladybug helped me to heal by mirroring for me my unhealthy behaviors and bringing attention to them. As I helped her change, so did I.

We are both more confident in new settings and we can go to the bathroom in public places now. I used, and still use, all the tools outlined in this book. Was that TMI? LOL.

What I did was create an **Image-Emotion Set™** of her confidently doing her business and me feeling so happy that she felt safe, secure, and grateful for her swift response. Things really changed for her and me. I let her sniff and mark around our entrance (her home), and then we would go for a walk. I instruct her when it's time to poop, and she does her business quickly and confidently.

For me, I have noticed that I am not as fearful of leaving the house and doing errands. And now I am ok with using public bathrooms if need be. I did not specifically "work" on these issues for myself; they just changed as I helped Ladybug to change.

*****

An indication that a pet is doing a job they are not meant to do is when they become aggressive toward other people or animals. They are generally taking on a job out of fear for their survival and that of their humans.

For example, if a naturally submissive pet feels that they must take on the role of the alpha, then they react fearfully and experience discomfort. Aggression is a common result. Because this role is not a job they are naturally aligned with and programmed to do, they become insecure and lose confidence in themselves. They lash out instead of responding calmly with curiosity. And when their alpha becomes worried, frustrated, fearful, and angry, it all gets worse.

If the images going through our minds are of the things we don't want them to do along with those **Low Vibration Emotions**, it becomes very confusing for our besties.

A submissive animal would be a nurturer like an emotional support dog (ESA) or therapy animal—not an alpha. The message for their humans is usually to take control of their own lives. There may be boundaries that need to be set or possibly a relationship that needs to end because it's unhealthy. They are training their humans to be alphas. By practicing being an alpha with our pets, we all gain confidence, and things naturally change in our lives too.

How would you feel if you were told that tomorrow you would become CEO of Apple Industries? You are thrust into a job that you know nothing about, and it is important to do it well for you and your family's survival; that's how our pets can feel. It's like the boss who is angry, condescending, and attacking because they're not confident in their ability to manage. They use intimidation instead of encouragement and our pets act the same way.

If your pets' job is to be the shaman healer, then their message to their human is that they need to become the confident leader and healer they are meant to be in their own lives. When we help our pets become confident in their natural jobs, we become confident and aware of ours too.

Let's talk about separation anxiety. If you have a pet with separation anxiety, then answer these questions:

- When do you start worrying about leaving them when you're going out?

- Are you visualizing past messes they have made with fear of them doing it again?
- What are you imagining and feeling as you're leaving your home?
- What do you think about while you're away?
- What do you visualize, and how do you feel when you're coming home?

In all your answers to those questions, could you say you had images and emotions of what you wanted them to do and feel? Were you feeling high or low vibration emotions? Were your thoughts mainly focused on what you were afraid, angry, or worried about, based on what they have done in the past?

Were your emotions **low vibrational frequencies** (fear, anger, shame, worry, guilt) or **high vibrational frequencies** (gratitude, love, peace, confidence)? What messages do you believe you were giving to your pet about what you wanted them to do and feel?

Our animals do not decipher our emotions as good or bad or what we do or do not want them to do. Instead, they pay attention to the most intense emotions and try to figure out what image goes along with them. Remember the bats? They react or respond to us based on the images in our minds and the most intense emotions we feel at that moment. When our pets get confused, behavioral concerns can arise.

When we focus on the low vibration emotions of fear, anxiety, worry, guilt, and anger, our pets react by shrinking away. Those emotions are contracting and heavy. Our pets react to their survival instinct to protect themselves and their humans as they feel vibrational frequencies. Remember the spider's message about paying attention to the vibrational frequencies of the emotions around us, as they do with their web? Our pets react or respond to our emotional vibrations and frequencies. If we are willing to watch them, we can learn about what emotions we are experiencing most intensely and decide if we are showing up for ourselves the way we want to. If not, we can change with the help of our pets.

PETS PERSPECTIVE:

"OMG, my human's most intense emotions are concern, fear, anger, worry, and guilt (low vibrational emotions.) I need to protect my survival." Their fight-or-flight response kicks in. "What image does my human have? What do they want me to do? I will follow their instructions."

The most intense emotions win out, and they react with unhealthy behavior, which is usually what we do not want them to do. They get the message that there is something wrong, and they should react.

Example:

Your pet scratches up furniture or destroys crates while you are away. You're coming home. Are you feeling fearful that you will come home to a mess? Are you imagining past messes?

YOUR PET'S PERSPECTIVE:

"Oh, my human wants me to make sure that the couch is safe and comfy. For some reason, they are afraid of it." Or

"I need to get out of my crate because it is not safe, and my human is telling me to get out."

Often, the belief is that our pet is mad at us for leaving them alone, and they are taking revenge.

Animals don't think that way. They don't experience the time required to hold a grudge and want revenge. *They don't understand the concept of revenge*. They feel only pure emotions. They can, however, have PTSD and react to certain stimuli that set it off. This is what these undesirable behaviors can turn into. I call it a **Neural Rut**.

Our pets are proud of their accomplishments and believe they are doing what we want them to do; however, they are often confused by their human's low vibration responses toward their efforts.

There's a difference between a **Reaction** and a **Response**. Our pets react to low vibration emotions with behaviors that move them away from the source of those emotions or to protect themselves and their humans. Our pets respond to high vibration emotions by drawing near and feeling confident, curious, and safe.

Behavioral issues can become a vicious and ongoing cycle of frustration for everyone. Our pets want more than anything to make us happy and do what we want them to do. They just can't figure it out—and honestly, sometimes I can't either. *Another important message we can learn from this is to clarify our intentions.*

The reason that **Image-Emotion Sets™** can work so well to help change these behaviors is they create a new response option for our pets.

What is very helpful here is that our pets will ALWAYS respond to high vibrational frequencies over the low ones.

When we use this tool, we are providing 30 seconds of high vibrational emotions (frequencies) and telling them exactly what we want them to do by creating the right images. Our pets can understand that.

The longer the undesirable behavior has been going on, the stronger their PTSD reaction becomes. The **Image-Emotion Sets™** and healing tools I am giving you will help. If this is the case with your pet, they will likely need more assistance to change these behaviors. They will need neural pathway restructuring, professional training, and perhaps medication.

Remember, if you already knew the solutions, it would not still be a problem. It's ok to reach out for help; that's the point of being human.

Our pets are telling us what we need to work on based on their behaviors. *They are training us to do the healing work on them that we need to do for ourselves.*

Rescue pets usually come to us with another set of messages as well. I believe they assist us in learning what our **Life Purpose** is. They come with behavioral and/or health issues, so we can learn the tools to help them and then use these tools with ourselves and others. That's how they help us find our **Life Purpose Healing Paths**. These are the paths that we are meant to walk and that bring us joy instead of pain.

If your pet is struggling with undesirable behaviors, try the following techniques:

Use your go-to **Image-Emotion Sets™** and add one or two more for a specific behavioral problem. It is best to work with one behavioral issue at a time.

Try these two **Image-Emotions Sets™**

1. One snapshot image of your pet doing what you want them to do with all the joy and happiness of them doing it.
2. Create one snapshot image of what it would look like for the problem to be resolved with all the joy and happiness of how that would feel.

Bounce between these and your go-to **Image-Emotion Sets™** that we have already created. Do this several times a day and work with this over the next three months.

The best time to employ this process is when we are visualizing and feeling the old low vibration emotions. Switch to the new **Image-Emotion Sets™** after feeling the old ones and consciously choosing to change them.

Our pets ALWAYS pay attention to the **Highest Vibration Emotions** because they are the most intense. When we add time to the equation, our pets can understand what it is we want. When we slow down our thoughts and emotions, our pets can catch up. Our messages become much clearer, and our pets can respond instead of getting confused and reacting.

Example: Separation Anxiety

You're leaving the house: **Image-Emotion Set™**

- Visualize an image of your pet snuggled in their favorite spot and feeling safe, happy, and loved.
- You feel happy, grateful, and relieved for at least 30 seconds.

You're coming home: Image-Emotion Set™

- Visualize an image of coming home to what you want to see.
- Feel relieved, happy, grateful, and excited about the change for at least 30 seconds.

Bounce back and forth between the two **Image-Emotion Sets™** before you leave, while you are leaving, while you are away, and when you are coming home. This will most likely take some time to get your pet to respond to your new **Image-Emotion Sets™**, so don't give up too easily. If you come home to a mess, it's best to stay neutral about it and clean it up. Think about something you feel grateful for in your life. Then redirect them to do something that you can praise—*and then praise like crazy!* Give them as many opportunities to feel confident and on the right track.

We want our pets to get used to an entirely different set of images and emotions. Give them time to adjust and keep it up. The more consistent we are, the less confusing it is for our pets. The **Low Vibrational Frequency** neural ruts that form can still be triggered under certain circumstances. By using these tools, the goal is to redirect that reaction into a response by creating new **High Vibrational Frequencies** pathways that can take over. We can do this with **Image-Emotion Sets™.**

Remember, it's important to visualize just one image at a time of what we want our pets to do and feel it for at least 30 seconds. The more we do this throughout the day, the more our pet will identify and respond to what we really want. Go from one **Image-Emotion Set™** to another. As we create more, they will string together and become a high vibration intuitive language, and the communication between us will improve. Our pets will feel more confident and become curious, which is a response, not a reaction.

Let's talk about neurological deficits and PTSD trauma next.

"Our animals, pets and wild alike, need our help to clear the energy they absorb from us and from the world, balance their energy for healing to happen, and provide healing for the damage that has already been done."

7

NEUROLOGICAL DEFICITS & PTSD TRAUMA

Animals can have neurological deficits and chemical imbalances, just like we can. This healing process requires additional tools added to the ones I have discussed so far. They require an advanced tool set and it's a good time to consult a veterinarian, pet psychic-medium, behaviorist, and trainer for guidance. I suggest interviewing different ones and researching their specialties. Ultimately, it's us who decide what is working or not.

I'm not going into the details of all these tools, as it's best for our pets to have someone else guide us with this healing process. I reach out to others when a problem arises with Ladybug.

It's important to find a veterinarian that is in line with your belief systems and is open to a holistic approach. I also recommend looking for other professionals if your veterinarian does not offer these types of holistic services. Utilizing some or all these services can be very helpful: Acupuncturist, Chiropractor, Behaviorist, Nutritionist, Flower Essence, and Supplement Expert.

When we work with a holistic veterinarian, they can guide us to what modalities would be most helpful. Some pet specialists will do muscle testing. This is a process where a trained professional uses kinesiology to assess muscle response to determine the causes and best treatments for our pet's needs.

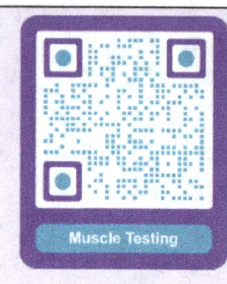

Muscle Testing

Diane Kazer at CHI Holistic Health Institute

Watch this YouTube video showing muscle testing being done for chiropractic treatment.

Use your camera to scan the QR code to explore the information

I've noticed that some of my clients experience guilt that they cannot help their pets more, especially if they have training in energetic healing modalities. Think of it like this: a therapist will not be effective doing therapy on their family members, and a surgeon does not operate on their family members either. We are not expected to be everything to our pets, sometimes, we need help from others. Remember, we are empathically entwined and struggling with many of the same issues that our pets have, sometimes, a different perspective can be very helpful.

Plus, these are tools that our pets are teaching us. We learn new tools that will help us in our lives alongside helping them. In fact, it's witnessing the new tools work on them that builds confidence for us.

One of our pet's messages here is to let others help us. We can ask ourselves where we could let others help us more in our lives.

Neurological and chemical imbalances can be caused by many factors. Here are some examples.

- Emotional Trauma (PTSD Triggers)
- Birth Defects
- Head Injury
- Karmic Imbalances
- Legacy Roots
- Stroke/Vascular Issues
- Toxic Exposure
- And there are more.

Emotional Trauma (PTSD Triggers) Animals can suffer from PTSD just like we can. PTSD is a neural restructuring that our brains can go through due to life-threatening physical and emotional traumas—and often worsens with repetitive stress. It starts with a situation that invokes a fear for safety and survival. The actual brain changes and new neural pathways (neural ruts) form, as both human and animal studies have shown.

Check out these links to two informative publications from the National Library of Medicine. Use your phone's camera to scan the provided QR codes:

Human PTSD Mode

Use your camera to scan the QR code to explore the information

NIH National Library of Medicine
National Center for Biotechnology Information

Human PTSD

Animal PTSD Model

Use your camera to scan the QR code to explore the information

NIH › National Library of Medicine
National Center for Biotechnology Information

Animal PTSD

If our pet's survival was threatened in the past, their fight-or-flight response kicked in, and they reacted to the threat at that moment. A new neural pathway grew in their brain. This new pathway can become reactive when any kind of similar threat arises. If in the future there is a perceived threat, real or not, that pathway can be triggered causing our pets to react defensively. It's usually an overreaction to the stimulus. And the more it triggers, the deeper and more ingrained the reaction becomes. This is the neural rut I spoke of, and it becomes increasingly intense and difficult to reverse the more they are exposed to the triggering stimulus.

Example:

When we rescue a pet, and they want nothing to do with our other animals when we get home. They may act aggressively, withdraw, or pee in undesirable places. This could be a PTSD-triggered reaction. A possible origin of this PTSD-triggered reaction could be that another animal had attacked them in the past, and the reaction we are witnessing is what saved them from that threat. Now, they are "programmed" to react that way. When they see another animal, their neural rut automatically fires, and it's like a bolt of lightning through their bodies. It is over-reactionary and can be completely uncontrollable at that moment.

When we use the tools in this book, along with other professionals, as needed, we can change our pet's neural rut reaction into a new neural pathway response. We can help them to **respond in a healthy and high vibrational** way instead of a **low vibration reaction**. Our pet's brain chemistry and physical structure can change, so the PTSD-triggered reaction will no longer become activated.

A neurological or PTSD healing program needs to focus on specific issues and their solutions. These are different and unique for each pet and their human.

Sometimes, they may need what I call **Neural Restructuring**. I do this with meditation, sound healing, and High Vibrational Healing Tools. I will discuss two of these that you can use with your pets in Chapter Nine.

I believe some of our pets come to us to help us learn to **balance karma and transform legacy**. This is another reason why neurological dysfunctions can occur. They could be karmically created from their past lives. Our pets can come to us with specific issues because we share past life traumas with them, and we are meant to heal them in this lifetime together. Our pets come to us at certain times for specific reasons. This is a prime example of that.

Legacy roots are genetic, inherited and can be caused by traumas in our current or past lifetimes. There are some pets that we have a really special bond with—*that's what I call* **Karmic–Legacy Pets,** *and we have a strong spiritual relationship together.* We planned to connect in this life to clear, balance, and heal a specific issue during our lives together.

These relationships are meant to teach us that there is more beyond this lifetime because we are meant to stay Spiritually connected with them after they transition. When our **Karmic-Legacy Pets** pass, they leave a big hole in our lives. They create a space within us and fill it with unconditional love, forgiveness, joy, and gratitude. In Chapter Eleven, Grief, Loss, & Transition, I will go into more depth about the amazing gifts and messages these pets have for us.

Karmic-Legacy Pets are our greatest teachers. They provide us with the opportunity to use and build confidence in our natural healing abilities. Because of their deficits, we can discover so much about ourselves.

Animals are our healers, teachers, and are the shamans of the world. Sometimes, these pets have neurological disorders, health problems, and behavioral issues.

Rescue pets are a prime example of what I am talking about here. They come to us with all kinds of issues, and they do that to teach us how to embrace our life healing paths and learn more about our life purpose.

Some pets are mediums, and they can actually "channel" other pets and people that have passed. Many of these pets can have seizures or fast changes in their personalities. Some pets are protectors of ectoplasmic energy and can see Spirits. Does your pet stare at a corner or react to something that is "not there?" I recommend using both **Sage and Palo Santo** to clear the space and make your pets feel more comfortable. Make sure to open windows and do it when they are not in the rooms as the smoke can be irritating to them.

This is a good time to address **Essential Oils**; they are strong and should be diluted at least ten times when using them for pets. Please do not use a diffuser around your pets, as the oils can get in your pet's eyes, lungs, and water or food dishes—all of which can be very dangerous for them. Please get advanced training in using essential oils or flower essences with animals if you are being called to do so.

Some of the advanced tools I work with and teach my clients when neurological and chemical imbalance issues are present include:

- Psychic-Medium Support
- Spiritual Guidance
- Neural Pathway Restructuring
- Sound Therapy
- Meditation
- Gemstone Therapy
- Space Clearing and Protection
- And I recommend other modalities as appropriate.

My goal is to help get things under control and then create a maintenance program that we can use with our pets moving forward. In the next chapter, I will discuss health issues and provide some ways to help them.

8

HEALTH ISSUES

ALWAYS seek medical care from your veterinarian when any health issues arise—especially if they have not been diagnosed, suddenly appear, or get worse quickly.

Sometimes, it takes investigation to uncover and to get down to the core messages our pets are trying to tell us about their health issues.

* * * * *

In my practice, I have found two main messages our pets tell us when they become ill.

The first message is that someone around them is having the same physical issue, and our pets are absorbing and mirroring it. Most often, it's their main human, but it can also be another family member, friend, or animal. Our pets sometimes come into our lives to help us heal by absorbing our physical pains and illnesses. Think of them as physical empaths. They do this for us so we can become aware of physical issues within ourselves that may be known or unknown to us. They can help us to get timely treatment when we listen. They are giving us a paw by "shouldering" some of our pain and illness to prevent us from getting sicker. They are giving us <u>time</u> to become aware of the issue and respond with self-care.

*The second message is to help us become confident in our abilities as healers and find our **Life Purpose Healing Paths** that fulfill us.* Everyone is a healer in their own unique way. Even software engineers are healers by solving problems with innovative technology they master.

Healers take many forms, and one of our pet's goals is to help us fully become the healers we are, recognize our natural abilities, and become confident in using them. They want us to learn more tools that will help us understand and develop our own unique gifts.

Humans have specific natural abilities (**Karmic Skills**), and our pets help us understand what they are and how to use them *for the greater good of all*. I call these **Karmic Skills and Spirit Jobs**. Some call them their Life Purpose. Our pets help us get on the right path.

By using **Energetic Communication™** with our pets to help them heal, we can become more aware of how to use our skills to help ourselves and the world as well. That is what our pets want, and it is one of the reasons they came to us.

I had a client named Tanner, who was a beautiful Collie. He suddenly became lethargic, incontinent, and seemed not even to know when he had to go to the bathroom. He would be standing and peeing, not even knowing he was. He was not eating well, and he obviously felt awful. After making sure their human had taken him to their veterinarian for a medical evaluation and treatment, I started to do some healing work on him. The veterinarian found nothing wrong in his bloodwork and other tests. They could not understand what was causing this rapid decline.

I connected with Tanner in meditation. As I started to call his Spirit Animals to him, my dog Ladybug came into the meditation. I was not expecting that since this was the first time she did this. So, I went with the flow and let Ladybug take the lead. She took us on a journey to an altar in a forest and placed Tanner on it. She began to sniff every inch of Tanner's body and all around him. Tanner was simply lying there. I started to wonder if he was beginning his final journey over the rainbow bridge and transitioning from this world to the next.

I stepped back and just watched as Ladybug and Tanner's Spiritual Guides and Healers circled him. They made strange sounds. It was amazing to watch—I definitely learned a thing or two from them. Suddenly, a gush of fluid left Tanner's body, and after a little time, he sat up and shook his head. I was instructed to do my energy clearing, chakra balancing, and soul-part retrieval healings with him. I asked "the team" what the gush of fluid that I saw was. They said it was toxins that were causing the rapid decline in his health and needed to be flushed from his system.

Ladybug and I continued to work with Tanner and his human, teaching them tools and providing healing for the handsome boy. When I dug a bit deeper with his human as to what messages Tanner had for them, I discovered that their human had recently ended their round of chemotherapy for cancer treatment. And it was successful! Well, that made all the sense in the world to me when I remembered the gush of fluid that was released from Tanner's body. He had absorbed some of the chemotherapy toxins from his human so they could heal. Those toxins needed to be released.

Of course, Tanner's human felt bad and guilty that he became sick because of them. I helped them to understand that it was Tanner's job to be a healer for them. I explained they both decided to be in each other's lives at that time so Tanner could help them heal. This was a **karmic-legacy pet relationship**. He was acting as a filter for his humans so they could learn how to clear, balance, and heal the energy within themselves.

As Tanner's human started to use the tools that they learned, Tanner began to feel better and stopped having accidents—and his human was thrilled. The **HESU™ Tool** was very effective in this situation, as it created a healthy and collaborative filtration system to remove that which was harmful and replace it with healing for both of them.

Tanner was an older boy, so this gave him and his human an opportunity to enjoy the time he had left in his life. Thank you, Tanner, for helping me find one of my Life Purpose Healing Paths. You were and are such a good boy! He died about a year later.

Tanner's humans shared with me through this period:

Before reading with healing sessions:

> *"Tanner is having accidents in the house; has been doing so for months now. Vet ran tests; nothing found. Wondering why he's not able to hold his bodily functions. Whatever you can pick up is appreciated."*

After reading with healing sessions:

> *"Hi Patti, Thank you for your amazing message! I've listened to it several times; and have to say it gave me goosebumps, especially the healing he received from you, your dog & the Elders. He seems more relaxed and content; there has only been one accident in the house."*

> *"Thank you again for all the help you've given us; I am so pleased—it clearly has helped & made a difference. You are an amazing lady with a special gift!"*

> **Fondly, Joan & Tanner.**

In the next chapter, I will discuss the third tool in Energetic Communication™, which consists of High Vibrational Healing tools we can effectively use with our pets. These tools are very effective, especially with physical issues.

9

HIGH VIBRATIONAL HEALING TOOLS

- Vibrational Frequencies
- Gemstones
- Chakras
- Healing Pet

What do all of these have in common? The ability to affect our pet's vibrational frequencies. Human bodies function at a lower resonant frequency than our animal counterparts. **Resonant Frequency** is the natural frequency where something vibrates at the highest vibrational frequency possible without amplification from another source. For humans, it is around 68 Hz. Since animals have heightened senses, like hearing, vision, smell, and sense of direction, to name a few, their resonant frequency is naturally higher than ours.

Just by being around our pets, our resonant frequency—the natural vibrational frequency of our bodies—can increase by at least 10 Hz—

and it can be more! This is why therapy dogs can have such an impact when working with sick children and elders. They amplify their humans' natural resonant frequencies. Have you noticed how many people want to connect with your pets out in public? It's like getting an injection of joy from them. People feel better just to be touched and loved by animals.

Every time our pets encounter others, they empathically absorb some of their energy, and the other person absorbs theirs as well. One way to help our pets stay healthy is to work with **High Vibrational Healing Tools**. You do not need a lot of training to use them, and you may also feel better just by using them with your pet.

It's impossible to do it wrong. All vibrational frequencies always rise to meet the higher one. That's a relief right? The higher the vibrational frequency, the healthier we all become.

Our bodies and emotions have a range of vibrational frequencies, and so do our senses. Take sound waves for instance:

> *"Humans with normal hearing can hear sounds between 20 Hz and 20,000 Hz. Frequencies above 20,000 Hz are known as ultrasound. When your dog tilts his head to listen to seemingly imaginary sounds, he is tuning in to ultrasonic frequencies, as high as 45,000 Hz."*

The National Park Service
Use your camera to scan the QR code to explore the information

Frequencies

Yup, animals have superpowers. Their **natural resonant frequency** is always higher than that of their human counterparts, even when they are sick. Some animals also use lower vibrational frequencies for specific healing work.

According to many researchers, our emotional state can influence our and our pets' health, happiness, and safety. You saw in the chart for emotional vibrational frequencies in Chapter Three that Gratitude is 900+Hz, Peace is 600 Hz, and Joy comes in at around 540 Hz—which is where dolphins and elephants natural resonant frequency comes in. Think of watching them frolic in the sea. Does it make you feel joyous to watch them? Our dog's natural resonance frequency is around 500 Hz, which is Love. I hear all the time that people feel unconditional love from their dogs.

Cats are different. It's the power of their vocals that creates healing for us. For example, the fundamental frequency of a domestic cat's purr is approximately 26.3 Hz. Seems low right? That is because they are helping us heal the deep emotions of shame, grief, and other low vibration emotions we can store in our bodies. The vibration of their purr shakes up those dense emotions and helps free them from our bodies. They will also take on whatever vibrational frequencies their humans need for healing. Notice how you feel when they vocalize. These are the emotions they want us to pay attention to. Cats are versatile and ever-changing. Flexibility and grounding are always some of the messages they have for us.

It's physics and is called the *Law of Resonance.* The higher the vibrational frequency, the healthier the body and the closer it is to

Spirit. Since our body is at about 68 Hz and our pets are naturally higher than ours, we can use things like the HESU™ Tool, gemstones, and chakra alignment to raise the vibrational frequencies of both our pets and us.

Law of Resonance:

When two objects, people or animals come together, they both put out their resonant energy (vibrational frequency). The body with the stronger resonance will always bring the body with the weaker resonance up to match its vibration.

Lily Rose

Find out more about resonant frequencies and how you can use different stones and jewelry to change yours and your pets.

Use your camera to scan the QR code to explore the information

Our pets are naturally at a higher resonant frequency than us, so we alone cannot affect their health except to bring it down. That is why I said earlier that *we are the rain of our rainforest filtration system* with our pets. Our pets absorb toxic energy from us, and if we use the tools outlined in this book to affect a healthy change, we become the rain.

When we use the **HESU™ Tool,** the energy flows through both our filters; it becomes a new resonant frequency that is guided for clearing, balancing, and providing healing. This creates a healthy high vibrational filtration system. When we add gemstones and chakra aligning, we can start to heal the damage that has already been done and prevent more damage from occurring.

We can use this law to create health and well-being for our pets by using **high vibrational healing tools** with them. When two or more vibrational frequencies come together, they combine, causing the lower vibrational frequency to rise and the higher vibrational frequency to reduce. They meet somewhere in the middle, creating a new resonant frequency. It is always higher and healthier for us and our pets. This is a way we can promote healing and support their health.

So, let me show you how to use some amazing tools to help your pet raise their natural resonant frequencies and yours along with them. These tools will be so helpful if your pet is sick, stressed, anxious, or imbalanced. And if they are healthy and happy already, these tools can keep them that way. Just by working with these tools, our resonant frequency can increase as well. This is one of our pet's goals for us, and it's a job they take very seriously. So, let's jump in, shall we?

GEMSTONES:

Gemstones always have a higher resonant frequency than the physical bodies of humans and animals. They match our emotions and beyond. They can be used to clear, balance, and heal the physical, emotional, mental, and energetic bodies. We can use them to connect to our Spiritual bodies too.

Using gemstones with our pets is quite easy and fun. We can use the stones with a specific intention for clearing, balancing, and healing or to just give our pets a nice self-care maintenance session. It's all about our intention; *what kind of rain will fall?* The gemstones will respond to our thoughts and emotions. We can also just ask our pets' Spirit Animal Guides to provide what they need as we use the gemstones.

I will generally use a mix of tumbled stones that have many different resonant frequencies. I also use stones that I find on the ground during our walks. I call these **Mother Earth Healing Stones.**

I'll randomly pick three stones and place them on the ground for Ladybug to choose. I will ask her to choose the clearing stone. The first stone she sniffs, I pick up and pet her with it to clear her energy. If she doesn't sniff the stones, then she does not want energetic clearing at that time.

Next, I'll ask her to pick the balancing stone. The one she sniffs is the right one, and the remaining stone is the healing stone. If she doesn't sniff for the balancing or healing stones, then she does not want me to use the gemstones with her at that time. I may give her some different stones to check out just to be sure. We can set any intention. And we can also just ask our pet to pick the stone that represents what they need.

If your pet likes to chew on the stones, then just hold one in each of your hands to keep them safe. Then, ask the same questions and look for their reactions. The hand they sniff the longest is the one. If they sniff both back and forth, they want both used. If they look at you like you're crazy and walk away, they do not want any gemstone healing at that time.

On walks with or without our pets, we can ask Mother Earth to guide us. Ask for a clearing stone and then begin looking at the ground. The first one that draws our attention and fits in our hand is the right one to pick up and use. We can do the same with the balancing and healing stones. Or just ask what our pet needs and let Mother Earth guide us.

Why not always just ask Mother Earth? Sometimes, a focused intention is needed. For example, if our pet is having any health, emotional, or behavioral issues, using the clearing, balancing, and healing process works very well. Ask a stone to clear what is causing the issue, balance them for healing to happen, and provide healing for the damage that has already been done.

When we also create an **Image-Emotion Set™** of it working with lots of high vibration emotions and using the **HESU™ Tools**, we have a winning collaboration, and it is powerful!

How to Use Gemstones with Our Pets:

Pick a stone with intention, hold it and ask the stone to do whatever your intention is, and then pet them with it.

Examples:

- Clearing Stone: Ask that all that needs to be cleared for their highest good be clear.
- Balancing stone: Ask that all their energy be balanced for healing to happen.
- Healing stone: Ask that the healing that they need for their highest good be complete. Or
  Ask a stone to do whatever they need to be done for their highest good.

If the energy is too intense for them, we can use a surrogate **Healing Pet**. Later in this chapter, I'll explain what a healing pet is and how to use it.

This is only a guide. Use your own words to state what you want your gemstone to do for your pet. It's impossible to do it wrong or pick the wrong stone—*they actually pick us!* Your pet will guide you, so go for it.

Trust your intuition. Our pets also have this message for us, and this is a good training exercise for building confidence in our own intuitive abilities as healers.

If we want to use specific stones, we can easily look up the qualities of various gemstones online. Although there are different opinions of where to buy stones, I believe that there are no right or wrong places. I find or buy them as they draw my attention. Remember, they pick us, and our pets and Higher-Selves are happy to guide us if we ask.

I do recommend clearing and re-charging any purchased, previously used, and ones we have in our current collection before using them with our pets. The ones we find outside are already cleared and charged by Mother Earth's love and intentions for healing. After using the stones or crystals on our pets, they will always need to be cleared and re-charged before using them again.

There are lots of ways to energetically clear and charge our stones—I like it quick and easy. I place them in salt water—any salt and any water will do, for five minutes. The reason this works is because water has so many unique healing and clearing properties, and salt has an ionic effect that changes them to their full resonant frequency. Salt and water partner well and work fast.

On a special full or new moon, I may place them outside overnight for an additional charge. A good smudging with Sage, Palo Santo, or Sweet Grass will add a ceremonial property to the stones.

Here are some examples of specific resonant frequencies of gemstones that I like to use and are included in my Pet Communication and Healing Toolkit:

- **Amethyst - 963 Hz**

   These crystals' resonant frequency aligns with the emotions of gratitude, freedom, and empowerment. It's a good crystal to use for angelic healing, insight, and dream work. Many times, the energy is too intense to use directly on our pets. We can use a surrogate healing pet to represent our pet. We can hold this crystal when our pets are having "bad" dreams. Set the intention to calm their inner world. It's great to hold them when meditating and invite them in to play. It's an excellent stone for Sixth Chakra or Third Eye strengthening. We can hold it over our Sixth Chakra or Third Eye and sit quietly to receive our pet's messages—and for them to receive ours.

- **Black Onyx - 396 Hz or Black Tourmaline - 432 Hz**

   These vibrational frequencies are close to dogs' natural resonant frequencies and align with the emotions of love and joy. These are good stones to use for clearing our pet's chakras and their physical bodies of infection and illness. Also, it is great to use to clear and protect against spiritual and energetic attacks. They can draw out the blocked energy that may be causing health and behavioral issues.

- **Clear Quartz - 32,768 Hz**

  These crystals' resonant frequency is off the charts. It's a great one to use for communicating intentions. Use it to focus on specific areas of illness and injury. It will amplify the resonant frequency of other stones. We can hold it with another stone that we are working with while using it on our pets. It will amplify the effects we intend. It's also great for neural pathway restructuring, regeneration, and clipping PTSD pathways.

- **Howlite - 852 Hz**

  These gemstones align with the emotions of appreciation and gratitude. It's a good stone to use for healing physical, emotional, and mental traumas with spiritual energy from your pet's Spirit Animal guides. It's an invitation for their guides to help our pets. It welcomes their help and brings us awareness of the solutions and messages they are offering.

- **Jasper - Hz varies**

  A good stone to use for grounding and balancing the physical, emotional, energetic, mental, and Spiritual energy. Grounding and balancing of energy is required for healing to happen. Any Jasper will work. Let your intuition guide you when picking one.

- **Rose Quartz - 350 Hz**

  These crystals are aligned perfectly with Spiritual love. A good stone to use for heart healing through compassion and Goddess energy. It's good to use when there has been a loss in the family, like a human or pet passing, a child leaving home, or a breakup.

Kati Kaia

Kati Kaia is a nice online resource I found for crystal resonant frequencies that you may enjoy looking at.

Use your camera to scan the QR code to explore the information

These are only guidelines, and I have found that each gemstone has its own unique resonant frequency. Picking your three stones outside is many times more effective. The reason I like using the tumbled stones is because I do not know exactly what their resonant frequency is because I don't know what they are. It's just like when using the **HESU™ River of Possibilities Tool** to create space for Spirit to work—not knowing the frequency of a gemstone allows Spirit to guide our pet's healing for their highest good. By using stones that we are just drawn to and have no idea what they are or what their reported resonant frequency is, we open the door for Spirit to work their magic!

When we let Spirit know, we trust them and ask for their help, we are demonstrating humility. It says that we don't need to control everything, and things do not need to be perfect. This has been a wonderful concept that has given me much relief in my own life.

CHAKRAS:

Another way we can amplify our pet's resonant frequency is to work with their **Chakra Centers.** We will work with the seven main chakra energy centers in the body. Chakra energy flows in two directions and ignites the auric field (moonbeam filter) and **Meridian System**. The first and seventh chakras flow up and down while the second and sixth chakras flow front and back. We can set our intention to work with both flows.

Chakras are represented in different colors and are of different sizes at different times. And they can be blocked or opened wide. Fortunately, we do not have to know the right size; we just need to have the intention that they are of the right size for our pets. Also, it's important to know that we are only working with the seven most known chakras, and there are many more.

The charts that follow will also show a point called the **Soul or Spirit Point**. We can use this point during transitions. When there are sudden changes in health, behavior, or environment, we can help our pets adjust by using the gemstones here. It is an energetic center that connects our soul to our Spirit like an umbilical cord. It is a great center to work with when miracles and major transformations are needed. I always ask that Spirit guide the transformation to accomplish what is for the highest good for my client's pets and mine.

We can set an intention for our pet that their chakras be opened, cleared, balanced and set for their highest good. Then, move gemstones or our hand over their chakras, front, back, up, and down. When our pets turn their back toward us, they want us to work with their chakras. If they move away, they may not want that stone or area worked on— it's a message. We can use a different stone, ask them to pick a stone, use a healing pet, or do it later.

If you know about chakras and energy work already, then set your intention based on your understanding. If you do not know anything about them, no worries. I have included some examples and charts in the next few pages.

Our pets know what they need, and Spirit will always guide us when we ask.

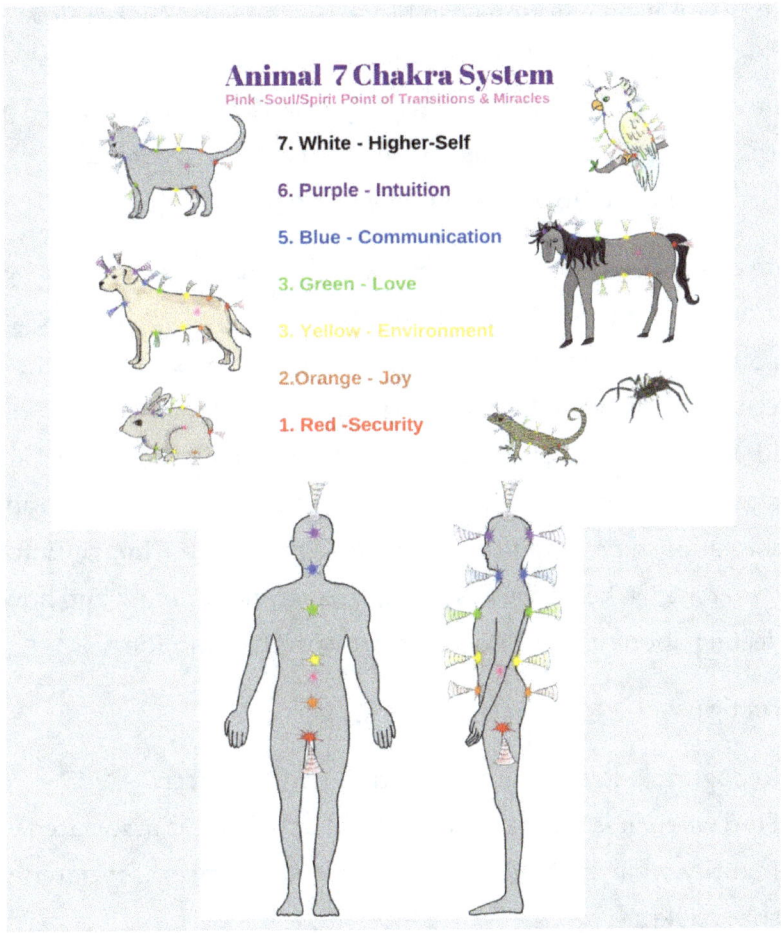

Another way we can work with our pet's chakra system is by paying attention to our own emotions. We can use our emotions to find and heal blocked energy that is causing illness and stress.

The chart on the next page indicates the resonant frequency of each chakra and the emotions associated with that chakra. The key to the right indicates the high and low vibrational frequency of emotions related to each chakra center, one and two, respectively.

The low vibration emotions can block that specific chakra flow. This can cause physical and emotional illness in our pets and ourselves. *Where chakras are blocked in our pets, they may also be blocked in us.* This is another gift our pets offer us. They can help us to clear, balance, and heal our energetic flow by working with theirs.

To use this tool, we can ask ourselves what low vibration emotions we feel most often during our day and not just the emotions we feel associated with our pet but throughout the entire day. Our pets give us hints that direct us to how we really show up emotionally for ourselves in this world. What is the most frequent low vibration emotion you feel about your pet? How often do you feel that same low vibration emotion in other relationships, situations, or jobs? Remember the **Image-Emotion Set™** exercise? What is the first image that comes to mind and how are you feeling about it now? We can start with this emotion.

Instructions:

- Recognize a low vibration emotion you feel often.
- Find where it is on the chart and what chakra it is associated with.
- Identify what high vibration emotions are also associated with that chakra.
- Create an **Image-Emotion Set™**.
- Visualize an image that makes you feel those high vibration emotions.

Follow this process:

- Move your hand over and around the specific chakra while using your **Image-Emotion Set™**.
- Visualize the image and feel the high vibration emotions for at least 30 seconds.
- You can hold a gemstone if you would like to amplify your resonant frequency.
- When you feel like you're done, then move your hand (gemstone) up and down the chakra system and say, "All (name) chakras open, clear, balance, and set for (name) highest good."

We know what we want to feel; the question is, how often are we feeling it? If we're willing to take stock and evaluate what we are, in fact, feeling most of the day, then we can change it. Ask yourself what repeated emotions drive you crazy all day.

Mine is frustration. OMG, it can push me right over the edge! So, as a result, I find a lot of "opportunities" to recognize and change this. It's associated with the heart chakra.

Remember when I was sharing my overwhelming frustration with Ladybugs sniffing, peeing, and pooping? She has guided me with her behavior to realize that frustration is one of my "go-to" low vibration emotions that I struggle with. Like begets like, and our emotions act like magnets. When I feel frustrated with her, I find myself in more situations that are frustrating to me. It can become a loop of frustration that never ends.

USING CHAKRAS & EMOTIONS TO HEAL OUR BODIES & PETS
We can use our emotions to find & heal blocked energy.

Identify a negative emotion you feel in list (2).

Choose a positive emotion in list (1), of that corresponding Chakra.

Place your hand or Gemstone over your's or your pet's corresponding Chakra.

Feel the positive emotion from your list (1) to unblock the energy flow..

7 CROWN 963 HZ
EMOTION 1000 + HZ
1. Connected, Confident, Clalm
2. Spacy, Insecure, Agressive

6 THIRD EYE 852 HZ
EMOTION 700 - 1000 HZ
1. Gratitude, Peace, Joy
2. Confused, Headache, Sad

5 THROAT 741 HZ
EMOTION 400 - 600 HZ
1. Hope, Happiness, Optimism
2. Lack Boundaries, Judgment

4 HEART 639 HZ
EMOTION 200-310 HZ
1. Courage, Willingness, Loved
2. Frustration, Stubborn, Fear/loss

3 SOLAR PLEXUS 528 HZ
EMOTION 150 - 175 HZ
1. Connected, Lucky, Social
2. Rage, Pride, Worry, Blame

2 SACRAL 417 HZ
EMOTION 75 - 125 HZ
1. Passionate, Creative, Playful
2. Grief, Fear, Jealousy, Desire

1 ROOT 396 HZ
EMOTION 0 - 50 HZ
1. Feel Supported, Safe, Grounded
2. Death, Shame, Guilt, Depression

1. **Emotions that will unblock and create a healthy energy flow.**
2. **Emotions that are causing blocked energy flows.**
   Use your negative emotion to represent your pet's

106

When I learned about this tool, things changed. I will now switch my emotions to high vibration emotions in the moment by using my "go-to" **Image-Emotion Set™.** I flip my frustration switch to the high vibration emotions of the heart chakra and in only 30 seconds my magnet changes and attracts willingness, courage and love.

I have found this very helpful in reducing my frustration manifestation. I have my "go-to" **Image-Emotion Set™** that makes me feel courageous, willing, and loved. I also look at the other low vibration emotions of that chakra and ask myself how these show up in my life. They are stubbornness and fear of loss. I see ways I can be stubborn, and I totally fear loss. I find myself "Waiting for the other shoe to drop." Now, I notice more often when I'm feeling these emotions and consciously change them by using my go-to **Image-Emotion Set™** over that chakra, sometimes with added gemstones for an extra boost.

I still feel frustrated, stubborn, and fearful at times. Now, I use this tool, and it helps me change those feelings before I create more of it. I notice that I am more courageous. I am willing to learn other perspectives when I'm feeling stuck and stubborn. I feel loved, and I notice the love others have for me instead of judging myself. I concentrate on the things that are moving me in the right direction instead of what I am doing wrong. *Better than I expected!*

Ladybug's health has improved and so has mine. Her last bloodwork showed improved kidney values and that is a rare occurrence. They usually just get worse. My gut issues and fear have improved dramatically...*yea!*

Ladybug is a good guide. I appreciate her patience, and I am willing to learn.

Our pets absorb **low vibrational energies** from us, and they react to the low vibrations with health, emotional, and neurological issues that mirror ours. They respond to our **high vibration emotions,** and this is one way to help them become and stay healthy, happy, and safe. We can use their **chakra system** to help restore a healthy energy flow, which facilitates alignment and balance for healing to happen by acknowledging our emotions.

Whenever we feel low vibrational emotions blocking our **chakras,** we can use the **Image-Emotion Set™** we created to flip the switch and create a new magnet.

Another way to work with our pets is by using what I call a Healing Pet.

HEALING PET:

Our pets are very sensitive to energy, and sometimes, it can be too intense for them when we first start using these tools. This is especially true when we start using gemstones and chakra healing. Also, when our pets are sick or have behavioral issues, we may need to start with a healing pet **"surrogate."** Our pets will let us know what they want by moving close or away. We can trust them, and we are not doing anything wrong.

A Healing Pet is a surrogate that we can make; it can be a stuffed animal, or we can use our arms. We treat the Healing Pet as if it were our own pet. We can use one Healing Pet for all our pets; we do not need a separate one for each. Simply decide the intention and which pet to connect with, and begin to provide healing on the Healing Pet.

When we want to use the Healing Pet, we can start by holding it and closing our eyes. We can then visualize all the **Image-Emotion Sets™**

and feel all the amazing emotions associated with each one we created. Just let them flow. Now you are talking! All our Image-Emotion Sets™ are turning into a string of high vibration emotions, and our pets feel them and see the images we are visualizing. This is the **Universal Language,** and it's powerful!

We are providing distance healing work that is activated with our **Image-Emotion Sets™** and intentions. If you know Reiki or use another form of distance healing, you can add them. However, you don't need advanced training for this process to work. Your intentions as prayers are fantastic, powerful, and enough.

We can use this technique while our pets are present or when we're separated from them. A Healing Pet is a good option for a pet that is fearful or aggressive and needs some personal space. Also, it's great to use when we are away at work or on vacation—especially for the pet who has separation anxiety and is really missing us.

I recommend using this technique when our pet is at the veterinarian receiving care. Pair it with an **Image-Emotion Set™** of gratitude and appreciation that everything worked out *better than expected!* Add the chakra work and gemstones too –

We can stroke the surrogate with gemstones as we would on our actual pet, as described before. Pick a gemstone to use based on intuition, its qualities, or feeling. Hold it while thinking of the specific pet. Tap the Healing Pet to ignite the flow. Move the stone over their chakras and any injuries while concentrating on the desired intention and positive outcome.

Using the same procedure as described earlier on a Healing Pet can powerfully affect its chakra system. We can also add the **HESU™ Tool** to the healing pet. It's a very powerful way for us to stay connected and heal together when we are apart. We can keep our healthy filtration system flowing. It works in both directions. Our energies are cleared and balanced, and healing is provided.

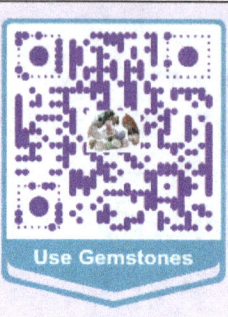

Using Gemstones with Your Pets

Watch these videos to see examples of how to use Gemstones with your pets. Ladybug is a great model!

Use your camera to scan the QR code to explore the information

I found this information while I was looking around on the internet, and I think it is so interesting:

> *"In 2003, Dr. Heidi Yellen ran a study to examine the frequencies of different fabrics. She used a machine called the "Ag-Environ machine," which had been used to measure the "signature frequency" output of plants and the human body.* **The machine's inventor, Bob Graham, found that the human body had different frequencies based on its level of health. The healthier the body, the higher the frequency.** *A healthy human body registered a frequency of 100, but a very diseased body had a frequency of 15."*

Yellen's study reported the following "signature frequencies" of different fabrics:

- Linen: 5,000
- Wool: 5,000
- Mixed linen and wool: 0... it appears that the frequencies cancel

each other out. Perhaps this accounts for the ancient instructions not to mix these fabrics.

- Organic cotton: 100
- Cotton: 70
- Silk: 15
- Polyester: 15
- Rayon: 15

Frequencies of Fabric

I just found this so interesting! Scan this QR code to explore this research more.

Use your camera to scan the QR code to explore the information

Fabric Hz

I have used this information to create a Healing Pet that is made up of this natural fabric and fillers.

MEDITATION AND MUSIC

Music and meditation are excellent examples of how different vibrational frequencies affect and can change our moods and provide healing for us and our pets. Sound is a collection of vibrational frequencies that can affect our physical, emotional, and spiritual bodies. They are measurable and have been associated with different stages of sleep and relaxation. Music is made up of notes that, when they are strung together, form melodies (Resonant Frequencies). When two or more notes come together, they form a harmony.

A harmony is a change in resonant frequency from the original two notes. We pick the music that aligns with the vibrational frequency of the emotion we want to feel. We can use music and meditation to help our pets relax, heal, and feel the way we want them to feel.

Meditations to Play for Your Pet

These are some meditations I created for pets. You will only hear the music, and your pets will hear the healing messages I am guiding!

Use your camera to scan the QR code to explore the information

SPIRIT ANIMALS:

Spirit Animals always have a resonant vibrational frequency—even higher than gemstones. Asking for their help will create an even higher vibrational frequency from which our pets will benefit. We can relax and not worry about doing it wrong—that's just impossible. When we invite a Spirit Animal to assist, we can be rest assured that they are guiding us for the highest good of all!

We set the intention we want to happen for our pet—ask your pet's Spirit Animal to guide the healing your pet requires for their highest good. Add any of the other tools described.

10

WILD ANIMALS

I must speak about the messages our wild animals have for us. The messages are there for us—if we listen. Typically, they show us where there are problems in the world that need to be fixed. Sometimes they will even give us the solutions. If we watch their behavior and how they change to accommodate for their survival, we can make similar changes to accommodate for ours. They are acting as mirrors for Mother Earth to help us learn. They can be our teachers if we let them.

Our animals are evolving just like we are. They want a stronger and more Spiritual relationship with us. They want to collaborate and play with us. They want us to listen to the messages they are sending to us in so many ways. Watching the news, I see more and more wild animals come to humans for help. Sea creatures entangled in nets, moose asking for help for their friends, and mothers asking for our help to save their babies. They are appreciative too. They often come back to thank the humans who help them.

Zoo animals are ambassadors for their species and also give us messages about the land they naturally inhabit. We can help them by clearing, balancing, and providing healing for them and their land. This is a gift we give them, and they can then use it to help their brothers, sisters, and Mother Earth.

I bring people to the local zoos regularly so we can provide healing for the animals there together. The animals do not want our **low vibrational emotions** of pity and guilt. They are not there for us to feel sorry for them. They want our **high vibration emotions** of gratitude, appreciation, love, and joy, along with our intentions for healing their land. They want to work with us to heal this planet in partnership.

I am not saying that all animals in captivity should be or are always being treated well, but in those cases, they really need our high vibration **Image-Emotions Sets™** and **HESU™ Tools** to help change the situation. And the humans responsible should be brought into the light and their actions judged. These animals are showing us where humans need help to grow, and we can appreciate them by bringing awareness to these issues so we can find solutions to them.

When we change our perspective to clearing, balancing, and providing healing in these situations while using these tools, things can change. I set my intentions to bring in the right people and to use the donations generated to create solutions for the highest good of all, thereby changing the energy of the situation. The low vibrational energy shifts to high vibration and that allows for Spirit to assist with solutions. This causes expansion and change. When we all set the intention that the right people, resources, and solutions are found quickly to cure the situation, powerful things can happen!

It sometimes feels impossible to change these things. First, it's important to understand the difference between energetic and physical change. Physical change is easy to see if we look. It's habitat improvements, the money donated, the people doing research, breeding programs, and so many more. Energetic change happens under the radar of human senses. It flows like a ripple in the water causing change as it flows in the most unexpected ways. We never really know exactly how the change will happen; however, we can be the initiation point! A prayer, a meditation, or an intention is all that is needed. We can be proud of our energetic donations to the cause!

The simplest way to do this is by using the tools in this book. Use the **HESU™ Tools** by visualizing with the intention of finding solutions for all animals, including their land and habitats.

Ground, Connect, and Filter—around all the animals and habitats.

- **Clear -** all that is blocking the solutions.
- **Balance -** the energy for solutions to come.
- **Heal -** everything needed to bring the right people, resources, and solutions.
- NOW!

We can create and use some **Image-Emotion Sets™** of them thriving, their land healing, and the right people making the right decisions for them! Create one where you hear that things are improving—*always better than you expected!*

We are making a powerful difference with energetic healing work. We are inviting Spirit to help and creating the space for them to work their magic.

The more we can give back to our pets and animals in the world, the quicker we can all heal. Feel those high vibration emotions, and let's see what happens!

"When we Heal our Animals, we Heal Ourselves, and together we Heal the World!"

11

GRIEF, LOSS, & TRANSITIONS

PERSPECTIVES IN HEALING

I feel that some of the most important work that I do is helping people through and after the loss of their pets. My clients often say the grief they feel is worse than if another person passed—and I agree.

I felt the need to include this difficult chapter because I have learned that our pets have so many messages and gifts that they want us to know when they leave us. I will share some different perspectives about the end-of-life process with those who have aging pets, those in transition, those who are grieving, and those whose pets have not come home.

Finding out the beautiful messages our pets have for us can be so healing. Their perspectives come from pure love and forgiveness. They give us gifts that can fill the big hole we feel in our hearts when they leave us. I hope that these perspectives can bring comfort, healing, and closure to those reading this chapter.

Let me share what all my animal clients tell me about this time in their lives (in addition, there will be references to them in this chapter):

- They feel our love and appreciate the care we give them.
- They love us and want us to always feel the unconditional love, gratitude, and forgiveness they have for us.
- They want to continue a Spiritual Relationship with us.
- They don't want to have treatments or interventions that we know will be stressful for them. No big tests.
- If possible, they want us to prepare and feel as ready as we can for their passing.
- They do not want us to feel guilty for decisions we make or do not make.
- They are concerned about our finances too. That sounds weird, right? Our pets do not want us to have that burden of debt after they pass. They say that it just adds to our pain. They remind us that they are at the end of life and will be entering their transitioning cycle. Spending more money and having more tests will not help them and will only hurt us.

In this chapter, I will share more of what I have been told from the pets and animals that I have helped through this process. I will also share what my pet parents have told me and some of their uplifting stories as well.

When a pet doesn't come home or dies unexpectedly, it can be a traumatizing experience, and it's easy to get stuck in what I call the

Grief Loop. When our pets don't come home, the loss is profound. There is no closure, and there is constant worry and ongoing hope. *It is torture!* There is a section at the end of this chapter where I will talk more about this and hopefully help those who have lost their pets in one way or another. It is possible to heal from this experience and find closure. While reading this chapter, embrace the perspectives and ideas that resonate with you.

We have a very different relationship with our pets than with almost anyone else. When they leave us in the physical world, it hurts a lot. Our pets are part of our daily lives; everything reminds us of them and how much we love and miss them. We miss their energy in our lives. We feel like a part of us is missing—and it is.

Our pets leave a hole in our hearts, and we need time to heal. In life, they filled us with love and made us feel accepted, even when we were at our worst. They loved and forgave us when we made mistakes. They supported us when we felt unworthy.

One of the gifts they give us is to increase our ability to receive love, forgiveness, and joy in our lives. Because of their love, a part of us expands. Our capacity to love grows. The love-hole they left now creates a space we can fill with more of what they gave us and how they made us feel when we are ready to receive them again. They made us more than we were before they came into our lives. They loved us for who we were: the good, the bad, and the ugly. This is why when they leave us, it can feel like a never-ending cycle of pain. *They give us so much.*

The love-hole can become an opportunity to add more to our lives as our beloved pets create space for us to embrace new opportunities.

They want us to choose the new things that will fill the love-hole with the same love, forgiveness, and joy that they once shared with us. However, this does not happen overnight and we need time to grieve.

Once we begin to heal, then we can choose to fill that love-hole with something new, something that brings us joy. Perhaps it's another pet, another chapter in our life, or an activity that we could not do before. This thought of "replacing" them with something new is, many times, the guilt that keeps us from healing and keeps us stuck in the grief loop. It's hard to know how and when to move into the recovery phase and allow new things to fill our love-hole. There is a beautiful ancient ceremony at the end of this chapter that can help with this transition for both pets that have passed and those who are lost.

As with any passing, there must be a time of grieving. The five stages of grief are *denial, anger, bargaining, depression, and acceptance,* although not necessarily in that order. We can become unable to move past the pain of our pets leaving. As a result, we do not receive the beautiful gifts that they want us to have, which can fill our love-hole, and this makes us miss out on the Spiritual relationship we can have together.

We certainly did not want our pets to leave us so we could have or do more, and we can't imagine replacing them ... *we just want them back!* Did we wait too long, or did we help them transition too soon? Were they in pain? Did we do something wrong? These are often the thoughts that keep us in the grief loop. We can think back and remember symptoms we missed that seem so obvious to us now. Hindsight is 20/20, and that could not be true here. It's hard to forgive ourselves when we think we missed something that could have made a difference. These are some of the guilty thoughts that keep us from doing exactly what our pets want us to do—live a life that is full of the kind of unconditional love, forgiveness, and joy that they gave us. *Our pets came to us for a time to help us love more—especially ourselves. They mirrored those emotions for us so we could learn we deserve them.*

After they cross, they are very excited to have a new Spiritual relationship with us, and they hope we will choose to have one with them. If we allow them to, they will give us messages that will help us discover the right paths to take. They will guide us and maybe bring a new pet, person, or opportunity for us to explore. They are happy when we are happy. The last thing they want us to do is hold onto guilt that we did something wrong. We all followed our **Pre-Life Plan** perfectly. We can honor their lives by becoming more because of their love.

Our pets want to build a strong Spiritual relationship with us, unlike any other. We usually trust them more than any other relationship we have. We know they would never hurt us, and they love us unconditionally. This makes them the perfect messenger from the "other side." If we feel them brush up against us or "see" them out of the corner of our eye, we can believe it's them! If we saw a ghost of a human or felt their touch, we would be afraid because we are not sure if they mean us any harm. We know our pets are safe and would never hurt us or put us in danger. They will always protect us, and we can trust that. We want to "see" them. We can receive messages from our pets, from other animals, plants, and Mother Earth. Our senses are another way we can receive Spiritual messages. However, we can talk ourselves out of it very easily.

Because of the Spiritual relationship that we can form together, we learn that there is indeed life beyond death, and it is safe. We can develop stronger Spiritual relationships with our guides, and that can heal our wounded souls.

Our pets will introduce us to more of our guides and **Spirit Animals.** We will trust them because we trust our pets and they will open a whole new world for us to get curious about and explore. Even if we already believe and have relationships with our Spiritual guides, our pets that have passed over can help us to deepen those relationships even more. It is a magical experience, and it is life-changing.

Another gift that does not feel like a gift at all is the gift of tears. It's counter-intuitive to think this way. Most of us have experienced loss in our past from losing a loved one, loss of other pets, relationships ending, or losing something dear to us. So often, we do not finish grieving those losses. We jump back into work and our routines too soon. We distract ourselves from the pain. We can also get pressured by others to get on with our lives. Generally speaking, the human race does not seem to value regeneration and healing time.

As a result, we have unresolved grief. It's like sticky goo in our physical and emotional bodies. There are specific ways to clear this physical "goo" so we can fully recover. These ways are through sobbing, laughing till we cry, sweating, and orgasms. When we are overflowing with "goo," our bodies purge it through both ends of our GI tract. To avoid that last one, we can utilize all the other ways of clearing this "goo" by expressing them all in balance. When out of balance, things like addictions, physical and mental illness, and, ultimately, the soul can go into darkness.

The gift of tears that our pets give us is actually the gift of sobbing tears to the point where our hearts hurt. We hit the bottom of our "well of grief," and we can clear all the "goo" from our past losses that we have not finished grieving. Oh, it sucks, it's intense, and there is no way around it unless we choose to stuff it back down again and move on with our lives too soon. Our pets hope we don't do that and instead use this time to clear the "goo" that is affecting us in ways we may not even be aware of.

The intense pain does end—I promise. We must give ourselves the time to grieve properly and let it all come out. We can notice the other memories of past losses we have experienced with gratitude for our pet's help in healing from them. The thoughts and memories can come up, and we can acknowledge, accept, and allow them to pass with some tears and gratitude. It is important for us to take off work and plan to be with those who support our grieving process without rushing us or trying to make us feel better but that is impossible until we get to the other side of loss and complete our grieving process.

The best way we can support our friends and family going through this is to listen and cry with them. Bring our favorite pictures and tell our favorite stories about their pets. Let them talk ... be silent and supportive when they sob. Just let them know they are loved, supported, and not alone. Call a spade a spade... *it sucks!* I'm crying right now just thinking about my pets that have passed.

When do we know we have come through to the other side of loss and our grieving cycle is complete? When we begin to cry and laugh while thinking about the silly things our pets did. When we feel the beautiful love they gave us with gratitude, and pictures bring a smile to our hearts. When we start to tell stories about them without crying, and we are ok when someone else is talking about the loss of their pet—that's when we know we are on the mend. If we are not getting to that point, then there is likely guilt locking us into the grief loop. I will go into all this more and share some ideas to consider later in this chapter.

PREPARATION

How on Earth can we prepare for our pets passing? God, that sounds awful. It's actually a very important step in our recovery process. When our pets are aging, we know the time will come when we must make some difficult decisions. I call this time the **Palliative Care Cycle: Care and Comfort.**

It's a time that we ask ourselves: how will we know the right time? Or should I get this expensive test done? What would they want? Are they in pain? Should I start this medication? This is emotionally a tough time and it's a hard transition. It's a difficult balance. I have found that this is the time when pet parents think back and see everything they did "wrong." It's where the guilt loop often begins.

We are doing the best we can and making the decisions that make sense at that time. We can always look back and think of ways we could have done things differently. There is no way to really know if those different decisions would have made any difference at all. This is the beginning of our pet's **End-of-Life**. I ask that everyone be kind to themselves. Be compassionate by asking how we would treat a friend going through this painful process and treat ourselves that way too.

We can create a plan with our pets to make that time special. We can heal from the loss of our pets and fill the love-hole they leave with the unconditional love they gave to us.

Medically, it's a tough time too. When we decide to switch to care-and-comfort, or "palliative care," it is good to let our veterinarian know. We want them to help us in providing care and comfort for our pets. I have found their guidance to be invaluable during this time. The focus of care shifts to pain management, nausea relief, disease management, and the aging process. Considering circumstances from a comfort viewpoint and not a treat or cure viewpoint helps lead to important decisions. What tests would be helpful for their comfort, not treatment, and medication changes may be made focusing on symptom relief rather than extending life.

A hard concept to swallow. It makes my heart hurt for all who have and are experiencing a loss like this. It's like losing a child, especially when they are our **Karma Legacy Pets**.

I ask myself, if the test showed something new, would I treat it differently? If yes, then I go ahead with it. If no, then I don't.

Then, I consider the current treatments and weigh my pet's comfort level with their stress level when receiving it. Which is less stressful for them? I've stopped treatments when I felt it was causing more distress or when it was time to help and support them in their transitioning process.

TRANSITIONING PROCESS

These are the hardest days. The physical dying process can look scary. All the cells in the body are dying. Sometimes, our pets can have seizures or difficulty breathing. Our pet's bodies sometimes look like they are in distress and pain. It's helpful to remember that our pets are not just their bodies. Their being and souls are who they really are. Their physical bodies, like ours, are just the suits they wear in the physical world. They have told me that their consciousness does not feel anything going on in their bodies when they are transitioning. Because they do not experience time, they do not "remember" minutes before and do not anticipate minutes after the present.

They know it's hard for us to watch this process. Sometimes, they stay until we are ready to let go of their physical body. This is when having a plan that supports our pets along with ourselves is important.

When our pets need help to transition, it's a difficult and guilt-ridden decision process. We know it's a merciful and loving thing to do. We question if we are waiting too long or not long enough. What do our pets want? How do we know when it is the right time? This can haunt people forever and I've learned that the right time is when we feel ready, as ready as we can be. This is their way of helping us to not hold onto any guilt.

I realize that when we start to ask ourselves these questions, our pets are not going to recover. They are at the end of their life cycle. It's not possible to make wrong decisions as to when to help them transition. There is no "too soon" or "too late"—the outcome is inevitable. Our pets will leave their bodies and come back to connect with us during this process. That is why it seems like they get "better" over time. They are ready when we are ready.

If you are at this decision-making point of end-of-life with your pet, here are a few things to consider:

1. Ask your veterinarian to help guide you.
2. Here are a few criteria that you can consider:
    *   Are they still playing as they did a month ago?
    *   Is it becoming increasingly difficult for them to get up from lying down positions?
    *   How is their mobility—can they still get up and down on furniture or stairs safely, if they previously could?
    *   Are they able to go to the bathroom normally, or are they having accidents?
    *   Do they look like they are in pain, and is it getting worse?
    *   Are they having difficulty breathing: too slow, too fast, or noisy?
    *   Are they only active when someone is with them?
    *   Have they stopped eating or drinking?
    *   There may be no change in the way they eat or drink all the way through their transition. This is a strong instinctual drive, but it is not always a good singular determinator.

When our pets begin their transitioning, whether it's from old age or from a disease process that takes them early, it's torture for us. Because they help us heal the unfinished grieving from our past, the intensity of our emotions is amplified. All our memories of previous losses we've suffered in the past begin to resurface . It can feel overwhelming and impossible to recover from.

It's normal and healthy to allow ourselves time to go through all these feelings and not rush them. People around us may want us to get on with our lives, to get rid of the things that remind us of our pets, or to get a new pet. They are well-intentioned; however, they don't realize that we are healing from all our past losses, and it takes time. So, we can take the time we need and do what we need to do.

Certain pets pass that will still bring a tear to our eye even years later. It's not a devastating cry like when they passed. This is a cry to release tension and heal from things going on at that time. Sometimes, we just need a good cry and are not able to get there, so they help us. I call this a **Maintenance Cry**.

I cried writing this chapter and I still have moments when I cry and laugh for the pets I've lost; however, I can move through it faster and find the joy in the new relationship that we have now. I am grateful for the Spiritual relationships we have created.

* * * * *

I have found that embracing different perspectives along with developing a Spiritual relationship is what has helped me and my clients to be able to fill our love-hole again.

Here are some more perspectives that pets have told me during their transition and after their passing:

- Animals are naturally Spiritual beings. They experience everything at once and they don't notice what is happening over time. Time is a human perspective. Because of this, when they are transitioning, they are not experiencing pain or suffering as we do. Their body may be experiencing pain or having reactions to the process. Our pets, however, are not. It's very difficult to watch our pets go through this process, and that's why they sometimes want us to help them transition. They have already assumed their role as our Spiritual Guides and are waiting for us to choose that Spiritual relationship with them.

- They also want us to know that when we think we see, feel, or hear them in the future—*we are!* They can descend easily to give us nudges, send us messages, and continue to build our relationship together.

- Animals do not understand guilt. They absolutely do not want us to feel guilty about their death and the decisions we did or didn't make. They understand it as the natural and predetermined life plan that we agreed to before we popped into this life together.

- Sometimes, our pets come back into our lives as other pets, babies, or other people, and sometimes, they have a different path and have come into our lives at a certain time for a specific reason.

- Pets never feel "replaced," and they want us to heal and fill our love-hole with the kind of love they gave us. In fact, they see it as creating space in our hearts to invite new and joyful things into our lives. They believe they opened a space that before them we didn't have. They see it as a gift they have given us. And when we heal from their passing, we can experience that gift again and again.

- Pets always tell me to tell their humans they love them. They want us to make decisions surrounding their transition by considering what will help us to heal after they have crossed. Our pets are only concerned with helping us do what is right for us and our healing, making decisions when we're ready.

That being said, it's still not easy to make tough decisions and help them cross the **Rainbow Bridge**. I do recommend talking with a pet psychic-medium that works with end-of-life situations, as it's very helpful to ask our pets what they want and to hear the messages they have for us.

After they've passed is also a good time to talk with a pet psychic-medium, especially if we're feeling overwhelmed and trapped in guilt that's keeping us in the grief loop I spoke of.

When we are faced with making these decisions, it's helpful to have an end-of-life plan. Instead of waiting and wondering when the time is right, you can set a date. It's never too early or too late for our pets. At this point, their passing is inevitable. We can create a loving end-of-life and what we believe they would want.

It's good to cry with them and be honest with them about how we feel. They want to help us, so they want us to be real with them.

Here are some ideas:

- Bring them to their favorite place. If they are weak, we may have to carry them or just drive to it and reminisce about the times spent there together.
- Spend time telling them the things we love about them and appreciating them, which is very helpful.
- Start a journal and write down the stories of your lives together. List the happiest times spent together, the cute little things they do, and the things that make us laugh. This list can be used to help us remember and feel the joy of their love again after they pass.
- Pull together your favorite pictures of them.

Decisions to make:

- When the end is near, do you want to have someone come to your home or you could go to your favorite veterinarian, if need be? If you want someone to come to your home, you'll need to contact them and see when they can come. Many times, they are pretty booked up and it can take a week or two. Remember, you can always schedule it, and then if you're not ready, you can reschedule.

- Do you want to bury them? There are pet cemeteries or maybe you already know the perfect place.

- After their passing, some people have their paw prints created on a card. Some people get tattoos made from the prints.

- Is there a blanket or a toy you would like them to have during and after their passing?

- You may want to have their ashes. You can have beautiful jewelry and other items made from the ashes to keep them close to you. I included a scan of a company called Spirit Pieces that I recommend below.

Spirit Pieces

Explore beautiful designs that can embody the magical relationship you share with your companion.

Use your camera to scan the QR code to explore the information

Many people want to give their pets their favorite foods. I caution you to only give them small amounts, as it can be very uncomfortable for them if their digestion is slowing down, as can happen during the transitioning process.

When the day comes, you can pick some soothing music, light some candles, and dim the lights. Many people like to open a window to help their soul release. You could use some essential oils, like lavender, to create a peaceful space. I like to have certain crystals and stones around that I pet them with. You can use the stones over their **Soul/Spirit Point** at their navel to invite their **Spirit Animal** to meet them. In Chapter Eight, there's a chakra chart that also shows this point. You can also open all their chakras to create space and balance for passing.

****

You can use other tools from this book during this time as well such as the **HESU™ Tool** and **Image-Emotion Sets**. Below are some examples. I invite you to use your own words if you'd like:

HESU™ TOOL—TRANSITION WITH CHAKRAS & GEMSTONES

Ground, Connect, and Filter:

While you pet them or use a stone over their chakras, and say:

- **Open** all (name of pet)'s chakras for their highest good.
- **Clear** all (name of pet)'s energy that needs to be released and returned.
- **Balance** all (name of pet)'s energy within, around, and between them.
- **Invite** (name of pet)'s Spirit Animal to guide them with love and gratitude through their transition gracefully and peacefully.

Image-Emotion Set™

- **Image** - Our pet is on the "other side"
- **Emotions** - Peace, gratitude, and love

When we create an end-of-life plan with some beautiful ceremonies, it can help us heal. We can feel good about the experience we gave them, instead of feeling guilty.

For those of you reading this book and are beginning, going through, or completing the end-of-life cycle with your pet, I have included my **Grief, Loss, & Transition Meditation Series**. We will not cross our pets by doing this program; rather, we will connect with them through love and peace. There is an introduction video and six meditations that follow. The meditations will take us from the palliative period, through transition, and building our Spiritual relationship together after they pass. There are also meditations to play for our pets that will help them relax and feel safe.

I hope they are helpful and bring the healing, peace, and joy that our pets want for us, through this difficult time.

Ladybug and I are so sorry for the loss you have gone through or are experiencing now, and we hope you can feel our love and hugs.

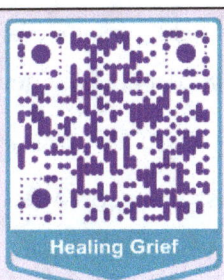

Grief, Loss, & Transition Meditation Series

We hope you find our Grief, Loss, & Transitions Meditation Series helpful and healing.

Use your camera to scan the QR code to explore the information.

Ladybugs Auric Energy Field

WHEN PETS DO NOT COME HOME

One of the most challenging situations is when our pets don't come home. It's excruciating because we don't know what has happened. It's usually a guilt-ridden time because we blame ourselves. Maybe the door was left open, or we let them be outdoor pets, or we weren't watching them, etc. There is always a unique situation and my heart breaks for everyone who has experienced this.

My cat Snowflake ran away when we moved to Massachusetts. We left the window open in the car when we got to our new home. We thought the smell of the unfamiliar environment would help our handsome boy start to adjust. We just left that window open a little bit; however, it was enough for him to squeeze out. We were gone for only a few minutes. We never saw him again. It was brutal; I was 13 at the time. I looked and looked. Every white cat I saw for years—I sought them out to see if it was Snowflake, to no avail.

Since then, I have learned a lot from pets who have gone missing. It's by far the most difficult session I provide. It's difficult because all I want to do is give hope and tell my clients where their pets are and that they are ok. More than anything, I want to help bring them home.

When I do a Lost Pet Session, I "see" through the pets' eyes. Animals cannot tell me what street they are on or how far away they are. Their viewing angle is completely different than ours. They also do not experience time as we do, so the images I receive could be from any time. The images could be from the first hours or in real-time from when they went missing—I have no way of really knowing. I don't lie, so If I "see" that a pet may have passed, I will always be honest. I am cautious about being concrete because I can and have been wrong, so I always preface my information with this.

When our pets do not come home, there is no closure. The first few months are a constant worry and search. The hope is that they are ok, and are safe and sound with someone else.

One very interesting perspective I have learned from lost pets is that they may have switched souls because their job with us was done. This is a strange way to think about it—let me explain more, and I hope it helps.

I was working with a cat that ran away. I sensed they were not coming back. I could not get a clear message about their whereabouts;

however, they were talking with me and giving me beautiful messages to share with their parents. One thing they have told me—and I always remembered was—*sometimes, an animal's soul job is done*, so they leave to allow for a switch of souls to take place. A new soul enters the body and is off to complete the new job they are assigned with someone else.

Sometimes, the lost pet's soul completes their life cycle here on Earth and is awaiting their humans to develop a **Spiritual relationship** with them. Sometimes, that is the reason they leave. I know this is difficult to believe. I had to wrap my head around it too.

Regardless of whether our lost pets return or not, they want us to connect with them in the Spiritual realm. Our pets are always connected to this realm. This is exactly what **Energetic Communication™** is all about. *It's always possible to stay connected and in communication with our pets—living, lost, or passed. This is the main message and gift they have for us.*

Sometimes, there are specific messages that a lost pet has for their family that have come up in sessions. Some of the common themes include:

- Their leaving was a pre-life plan before they arrived in their families' lives.
- They did not leave to hurt us or because they did not like us.
- Their family did not do anything wrong, even if an action could have been prevented. It was the pet's choice, and it was their time to leave or to enter into a new job.
- They are sorry for the deep hurt they have caused.
- They want to communicate with their family Spiritually.
- They want their family to feel the love and gratitude they have for them.

- They want their family to forgive themselves and not feel guilty.
- They do not want their family to constantly look for them, as they will come back on their own if that is the pre-lifetime plan.

There are indeed times when an animal leaves a situation because it's abusive or traumatizing. If you are reading this and are devastated by your pet going missing, then rest assured this is not the case for you. You would be the one an injured and traumatized animal would seek shelter with. How do I know this? If you were an abuser, you likely wouldn't care if they left, and I would be very surprised if you were reading this book.

I feel confident in saying that if your pet is lost, there's a higher purpose. There is usually a Spiritual message that is different for each situation. This is a good time to seek counsel with a pet psychic-medium that specializes in lost pet recovery.

This is not my specialty; however, the emotional recovery process is. Please don't suffer alone. Reach out for guidance and new perspectives so you can heal from this devastating circumstance. Our lost pets want us to remember them with the joy and gratitude we always had for them.

Connect With Your Lost Pet Meditations

It is so hard when are pets are lost. We hope these meditations can help you re-connect to your loved companion and foster healing.

Use your camera to scan the QR code to explore the information.

ANCIENT HEALING CEREMONY

This is an ancient ceremony that marks the completion of grieving and begins the celebration of the lives that have passed. This can be performed for pets and loved ones who have passed. When we decide it is time to bring new love, joy, and peace into our lives again, we can mark this transition using this ceremony.

It's also a ceremony that can help those who have pets or loved ones who did not return home. It's important to have closure for healing to happen. This closure is one of acceptance, not forgetting. It's a message to our lost ones that no matter why they went missing, or what happened to them, or where they are now, we forgive them for leaving. Even when we don't understand why they went missing, we love and forgive them and ourselves, despite any mistakes that may have been made.

When we decide it's time to stop actively looking for our loved ones, it's a good time to do this ceremony. We're not closing the door or sending a message that would stop our loved ones from returning home. When we perform this ceremony, we are sending a message that we are accepting their path. And if their path is to come home, we will leave the door open for their loving return.

In either case, *we do not need to be ready—we only need to be willing.* This is a ceremony of transition. We can do it when we want to be ready. It can be done when we want to heal and don't know exactly how. We can also do it again if we find it would be helpful—possibly on the first anniversary of their death, the time they went missing or repeating the date when we did this ceremony for them.

This ceremony symbolizes the transmuting of our grief into the opposite energy of joy. It signals to our hearts that we are now ready to fill that love-hole our loved ones left in our souls with the kind of love, forgiveness, and joy they gave us in this world.

Inviting others to attend the ceremony can be very healing—or we can let it be special for just us. Fire is a required element. Fire is the ultimate transmuting force. Fire changes the form of wood into ash, heat, color, smell, and smoke. All these forms have the same fire energy exchange, yet they all carry different effects. Transmutation causes changes in the energetic and molecular structure.

Our emotions have an equal energy exchange, too: opposite and equal intensity. We can transmute our sorrow, anger, fear, depression, and sadness (the wood) into happiness, joy, peace, and gratitude (ash, heat, color, smell, and smoke). When our conscious and subconscious can realize and accept the transmuting of emotions, they can help us to heal. This ceremony helps to facilitate healing and closure. It can be a turning point when we are willing to receive unconditional love and end our grieving cycle.

Ceremonial Procedure:

Begin by finding your favorite pictures of your pet (or loved ones). Get a notebook and start writing down stories you remember that made you laugh, feel loved, and supported. Ask others who may be joining you to do the same.

Build a fire if you are able, or you can use a special candle. Pick an item of theirs or write their names on a piece of paper that you will throw into the fire or burn in the candle. You can include a message if you like.

Sit around the fire or candle with your friends and family or by yourself. Look at the pictures and read the stories you wrote. If you are with others, it's helpful to have an item that is passed around. When someone is holding it, it's their time to talk and share. When they are finished, they will pass it along to the next person. It's not necessary for everyone to talk and share. They can listen. Let people know they can just pass the item to the next person. This is inspired by a Native American tradition of using a **Talking Feather**.

When ready, throw the item or paper and message into the fire or let it burn in a candle flame.

Everyone sits quietly and watches as the item or paper transmutes into smoke and ash. *Smell the aroma of messages of love. See the beautiful colors representing the beauty of our love.* We also send messages that we are willing and ready to begin receiving what will fill our love-hole with love, joy, and peace, guided to us by them.

This is not a ceremony to forget or replace pets, it's to honor the love they gave us and to demonstrate that we are willing to receive their wishes for us to experience their kind of love again.

Make sure there are tissues available for all. It can feel overwhelming. Remind everyone that they are in a safe space and they are supported. They are free to step away and come back when they're ready.

It's important to check in with ourselves and others the next day and offer support, discuss the ceremony, and make plans to go and do something that is fun together. That's what our pets want.

12

ANIMAL STORIES

CLIENT STORIES

Cannoli & Tootsie

This story amazed me. It's a karmic relationship that has evolved. When I work with a family, their pets tell me what they want their humans to know. I sometimes find it's not always what they want to hear; however, this one was, and it's heartwarming.

Angela came to me because she was having difficulty healing from the recent transition of her canine bestie, Cannoli. It was a joy to connect with her two dogs—Cannoli and Tootsie.

I explained that we are meant to carry on a Spiritual Relationship with some of our pets and that she was meant to keep contact with these two special pups. Karmic pets sure leave a love-hole when they leave this physical world. Shamans say that we lose a part of ourselves through a difficult process and that sometimes a "Soul Part" needs to be retrieved. This story is evidence of that happening.

Angela's pets told me some great stories that made us laugh; they have a great sense of humor! Toward the end of our session, Cannoli started to "shake" me. I felt like electricity was going through me. He told me he was coming back to her; he was coming back as her baby!!! I did not want to say it out loud—I never want to give false hope. I heard "Pick a stone," so I immediately did, and when I looked at the stone that I picked, there was an image of a human baby in a womb with an umbilical cord. I knew then I had to tell Angela.

Cannoli said he was coming back as your baby. This was amazing for so many reasons, so I shared the news with her. She told me that her doctors said she could not have children. I told her that I was not always right and did not want to give false hope. A few days later, she texted me with the happy news—she was pregnant! I was so happy for her and her growing family.

> *"I love Patti, what a wonderful soul she is. I recently had my dog pass, and she gave me great guidance on overcoming such loss. She was able to connect with him and share some memorable moments we had together. She also was able to communicate with my other dog who is still with us, and wow was she right! She also mentioned my passed dog was going to be coming back to me as my child and two days later I found out I was pregnant. Thank you Patti, I feel so happy."*
>
> ♥ *Angela Ferrecchia*

Cannoli (White)
& Tootsie (Brown)

The Fox and the Dog

At one of the psychic fairs I was doing readings at, I met a woman who was having difficulty with her dog. He had suddenly become fearful of going outside. She could not understand why. She had not changed anything that she could think of. He did not have a bad experience.

When I asked her pup, he showed me a picture of a fox. He said he was afraid to go out because of the fox. When I shared this information with his human, she was very confused. She said there were no foxes around where they lived, and there was a fence that she did not believe a fox could climb. I told her that sometimes this happens, and I encouraged her to let the message come to her over the next few weeks. I also told her that I was not always right and could have picked up information from someone walking by. She went on her way.

I saw her several months later, and she was excited to tell me she had figured out the fox message: she had been spreading fox urine around the foundation of her home to keep small animals out. We had a good laugh. She did stop using the fox urine and her pup started to go out again without fear. I still laugh when I think about this story!

Jake & Boots

The family of Jake and Boots came to me because they had lost one of their other dear cats a few months back.

They had recently brought Jake into the home. He was an older cat that had only been with two humans in his life. His first human had to give him up due to health reasons and a family member took him in. However, they had two dogs that always barked at him. One day, he escaped outside and got into a fight. He had some wounds that required treatment. The family took him to the vet and did not take him home. He was rescued by a no-kill shelter.

Jake was rescued and found his forever home with his new pet parents and brother, Boots. Boots was a submissive boy who was still grieving the loss of his alpha-kitty upon Jake's arrival.

Initially, when I connected with Jake, he told me he was terribly confused because he did not know what his name was. When I asked his family about this, they told me they had been trying to figure out if they should call him Jake or Jack, and they were calling him both to see what he liked. I told them to pick a name and that their new boy liked Jake. So, Jake it was!

During our first session, Boots came to me and told me he was sick. His stomach and back did not feel good at all. Animals typically do not show symptoms until they're really bad, so his family didn't know. I asked them to take Boots to his veterinarian for a thorough check-up, including bloodwork. They did and found out he had cancer. It was early enough that the chemotherapy they started gave them another seven months together.

Boot's family showed him the amazing love and care that they so naturally give to all in their lives. Boots always told me how much he appreciated the amazing care he received. He said he felt loved and loved his pet parents so much. He was glad that they developed their Spiritual relationship together during that time.

Jake was having some difficulty adjusting to his new home. He would bite and scratch his new family and chase poor Boots around aggressively. The problem was that Jake would come to his humans acting like he wanted to be petted and, after a short time, would turn on them ... *And he could cause some damage!* He sent his mom to the hospital a few times for antibiotics. I thought Jake may have to leave the family if he did not stop this behavior. However, Jake's family was very committed to him and were determined to make it work and help him heal.

First, we had to get Jake to stop being aggressive toward sweet Boots. After explaining to him how sick Boots was and that he needed to rest, Jake started to understand. He sensed how sick Boots was and his natural survival instincts triggered him to kick the sick member of their pride out. This is a common occurrence in packs and prides in the wild to maintain group strength and security. The food should go to the healthy members, not wasted on the sick ones. It is a healthy and natural response.

Jake needed some neural pathway restructuring with a DNA shift to disconnect this instinctual trigger. I created some meditations for his family to do with him to clip and replace these pathways with a more domesticated and nurturing neural network. This really helped! We also used this technique with Boots to curtail the progression of his cancer and relieve discomfort.

Jake had messages! He was a medium, meaning he could talk with (channel) humans and other pets that had passed. He would channel the cat that had transitioned before he came to the family. While channeling this cat, he wanted to be petted. When Jake "came back," his ears would flick, and he was surprised to find himself being petted, and then he would attack. His family began noticing and would honor his ear flicks by moving away. This definitely helped everyone!

Jake had a very strong hunting drive, so his family wisely enlisted the help of a behaviorist specializing in cats. They suggested limiting his time in the window watching other animals. This could ignite his hunting drive and trigger aggressive behavior. They did this and got him all kinds of fun stuff to play with, and he loved it. His drive subsided quite a bit.

Jake did keep biting his mom, however, and sometimes hard. After several months, he told me that he wanted his mom to set more boundaries and do more self-care. This is a common message our pets have for us, including mine. Jake said he would nip her, and then if she did not listen, the bites would get harder. He came to the family to help his mom learn and gain confidence in her natural Spiritual skills as a healer. He presented her with lots of opportunities to learn! As she started to stop and consider what was going on in her life, set healthy boundaries, and do more self-care, Jake only had to give a quick nip. Ok, we can deal with that, hahaha. Jake also had many messages for his dad, too.

I was honored to work with Jake and Boots' family for about a year, and was amazed by the growth, love, and compassion they showed. They're wonderful. I provided regular clearing, balancing, and healing for the whole family during this time and guided them with meditations, tools, and resources.

Boots passed away, and because his family used the tools I suggested and heard the messages he had for them, they received the beautiful gifts he had to share. They created a plan for his transition that they felt he would want. They gave him a beautiful and healing transition with the expectation of continuing to build their Spiritual Relationship together.

> *"Patti is amazing. She is accurate, compassionate, kind, caring and patient. I first reached out to Patti because our newly adopted cat Jake was having behavior problems. During our first session I learned that our other cat Boots was not feeling well and terminally ill. Boots communicated that before he showed symptoms. We were floored*

and I was devastated. Patti helped us through the process of palliative care and saying goodbye. Patti helped my husband and I learn how to communicate with Boots and Jake and also helped them navigate changes to our household. She gave us tools to use that helped all of us. She is kind, compassionate and caring.

She helped prepare us and learn the lessons Boots came to teach us as he transitioned over the rainbow 🌈 bridge. She gave us tools to help Jake and his behaviors and understand what his lessons are for us."

Anne Quemere

Jake

Boots

Sugar and Knight

I did a communication and healing session for two dogs named Sugar and Knight. When I connected with them, I got scolded by Sugar. She wanted to know who I was and If her parents knew I was talking to them. She refused to talk with me. Knight, however, was excited for his healing and asked her to let me do it. Sugar reluctantly allowed me to, under her supervision. It was then I learned a very important lesson. I needed to make sure that the parents I work with let their pets know it's ok to talk with me. I think that makes sense and I was appreciative of the lesson.

Sugar's mom let her know it was ok to talk with me. Sugar still didn't trust me and only let me do a little work with her at a time.

One day, a few months later, I was driving home from a long day of visiting nursing. Sugar came to me, and she was upset, to say the least. She was so upset that I had to pull over and go into meditation to talk with her immediately. I was literally shaking from her energy. When I connected with her, she started to yell at me that her mom needed to go to the veterinarian. I was confused—was Sugar hurt or sick and mom needed to bring her? Nope, she said mom needs to go—something is really wrong. I came out of meditation and called her mom right away. I asked her if she was ok and told her what Sugar said. Her mom laughed and said she had back pain all night, and her husband wasn't home. Her husband could help her relieve the pain, but since he was not home, Sugar thought it was her job. She did not know what to do. Sugar was so upset and concerned about her mom. Her mom told me that Sugar would not leave her side all night. I realized that Sugar meant that her mom needed to see her doctor; however, she did not understand that humans saw doctors—not veterinarians! After that, Sugar trusted me and her mom was ok.

Sugar has left this physical world, and she still lets me know she is watching over her mom. I will see her in a cloud or the fog on the window and take a picture to send to her mom. She'll give me messages to deliver to her mom at just the right time, right when her mom needed them most.

Thank you, Sugar, for the wonderful lessons, and I am so grateful for our ongoing Spiritual Relationship. Love you too, Knight.

"Working with Patti has been absolutely amazing! I have worked with her for years now and I am so humbled to be able to connect with her and her healing art. She is incredibly kind, transparent and supportive.

During a difficult time losing my pup, she was able to connect me with an abundant amount of healing I needed! My Sugar loves to connect with Patti and I enjoy hearing about it. Even prior to the loss of my pup Patti has given me great insight into both of my dogs and helped us understand some of the needs they were already trying to communicate to us!

Patti has a wealth of knowledge, is so personable and such a genuine person. I am so grateful to have met Patti, connected with her and to have experienced her wonderful energy!"

Kayla Rosario-Muñoz

Sugar – White
Knight – Brown &White

Chloe the Grumpy Cat

Back in 2016, Chloe's family asked me for help. Chloe came to her family when she was a kitten. She had displayed aggressive behavior and fear from day one. She was older when I started to work with them. No matter what her parents and sister did, Chloe would not change her behavior. When her family tried to pet her, she would attack and bite them, sometimes drawing blood. Goodness, we needed to find out why this was happening quickly for her family's safety; they were so worried about her and felt so bad they could not help her feel comfortable, safe, and loved. Chloe said she did feel safe and loved. She appreciated all the effort her family was giving her. However, she was not comfortable.

I connected with beautiful Chloe and found out some amazing reasons for her behavior and some solutions she offered for her family to implement. First, she told me she could not see well. It was with her that I learned that our pets could have past lifetimes, just like we can. Their past lifetimes are guided by Spirit Animals. She had two different lifetimes that were influencing her vision and causing her to feel confused.

One lifetime was a dolphin, and the other was a wild cat. She was seeing through one eye of her Cat Spirit Animal and out of the other her Dolphin Spirit Animal—as a result, she could not perceive where objects were in front of her; for example, out of one eye, she would see a hand coming down to pet her, and it would be a foot away; however, out of the other eye, it would be six inches. Can you imagine how disconcerting that would be? It freaked her out, and she would attack, scratching and biting to figure out where the object was. The other issue was around corners. Her perspective was off, and she could not judge where they were and would often bump into them. She became fearful of jumping and climbing because of her double visual perspectives. These things embarrassed her. Cats pride themselves on their ability to have a bird's eye view.

Chloe talked to me about strange lights that twinkled and gave her headaches. When discussing this with her family, I found out that she was talking about sequins and glitter. Her human sister loved to dance and had lots of sparkly outfits. She also loved getting Chloe toys that sparked and wondered why she did not want to play with them.

I asked Chloe for some solutions that her family could do for her. I told her she had to stop biting because it was hurting her family. Chloe did not want to hurt anyone and gave me instructions to share.

1. When they want to pet her, they need to get down on her level, hold their hand out lower than Chloe's head, and be still. She would come to them when she was ready and let them pet her chest and chin. This worked well for the family. Chloe still had some PTSD to work out, however, this was a great first step.
2. I told the family to walk around the home at her level to see her perspective. I asked them to round out the corners and furniture in her path, especially where they had seen her bump into things. I suggested they lighten dark corners. Chloe's family did this, and she was very happy.
3. Chloe said that her water and food bowls were in a corner, and she was afraid to eat when anyone was around. This really worried

her family, as one of the reasons they contacted me was her poor eating habits. I told them that Chloe wanted to have her back to the wall, not a corner, so she could see in front of her when she drank and ate. Her family did this, and her eating and drinking habits improved! Chloe also wanted to make sure her family knew the treats she liked, LOL.

4. Lastly, I told Chloe's family about her fear of sparkly things. Her sister was careful not to walk around and dance in the house with her sparkles on. They also got her some new toys, without shiny things. Chloe asked for mice because it was a form she recognized, and she could get some of her frustrated energy out!

Chloe improved and her family was relieved because now they understood why Chloe was acting this way. And it was not because they did anything wrong. They still needed to move slowly and consider how she perceived things. It was a relief for Chloe as well, and her confidence grew because her family listened and changed the things she wanted. It made Cloe more willing to become a cautious kitty instead of a dangerous one.

PERSONAL STORIES

Putzi

Putzi—My Protector.

When I was about five years old, I had a boxer named Putzi. She was my first dog, and she saved my life. Putzi also taught me that not everyone talks to animals like I do.

I was out playing in our front yard, and Putzi was lying down in the sun nearby. I saw something across the street and started to run across the road. There was a car coming. Putzi ran and knocked me down. She stood over me, glaring into my eyes. She was mad and I could "hear" her telling me to never cross the road without looking first and that she would show me how. I remember having an image in my mind of stopping at the edge of the road and looking both ways. Putzi then walked me to the road and sat down. She looked both ways and at me. Then we crossed the road. She turned around and waited for me to show her that I would look both ways and cross. Putzi was satisfied, and when we were back in our yard, she went back to lie in the sun again.

I was so excited that I told all the kids in the neighborhood that Putzi showed me how to cross the road, I even showed them how to do it. My friends told their parents ... and their parents became concerned. I was born in 1966, so can you imagine what they were thinking? I learned that most adults and many children did not regularly talk with animals. I kind of shut up for a while after that—LOL.

Snowflake—My Buddy

We got Snowflake when I was around seven. He was a great cat and, just like his name, he was white as the driven snow. I would go out and call him at dinnertime, and he would promptly return home. He would not come to anyone else, only me. I felt special!

He was an outside cat, and we never had a litter box for him. One day, he complained to me, saying that sometimes he was stuck inside and he would have to go to the bathroom. I thought about it and then told him he could use the toilet like me. He was interested as I showed him the way to the bathroom and demonstrated how the toilet worked. He was happy with that solution, and moving forward, we would find his contributions in the bathroom and sometimes the shower; both were just fine with us. He never learned to flush the toilet, even though I tried to teach him... haha. He was a great cat, and I used to call him my dog cat. He would follow me around, and I always felt safe and loved. He was the cat that ran away when we left the window open.

Sadie—My Little Miracle Girl

I rescued Sadie when she was three months old. She was the last one out of a litter of 12. Her mother gave birth to her in a barn, and it was cold. Someone found them and took them to a shelter, where I found her. She had neurological and chemical imbalances that caused her to have incredible anxiety and an incredible drive to chase and attack other animals. She would bark and growl at people, but she never bit. I was always worried that someday she would.

I call Sadie my little miracle girl because she literally saved my life. I was a paramedic at the time and was having abdominal pains. They were bad and getting worse. I fell to my hands and knees and could not talk; the pain was so great. I wanted to yell, "Call 911," but I couldn't. Then I saw Sadie; she stood in front of me, nose to nose, looking right into my eyes. I was crying. She then tucked her head under my chin and walked under me. I could feel her warm body against my chest and belly as she walked. I remember feeling her tail as it rubbed against my body. At that point, my pain was gone. I mean, completely gone! I knew she had helped me, and I was so grateful. It was then I really understood the healing power animals had. I did not understand until she passed that she had absorbed the pain from me. Over the next few years, she had to have three surgeries to remove benign lumps in the exact place on her belly where my pain was.

It didn't register for me that the reason she required three surgeries was because she absorbed my abdominal pain empathically and held onto it. When I started to learn about the HESU™ Tool, I realized that if I had cleared her, she may not have needed them. Oh boy, did I feel guilty! She went through all that for me, and I could have helped her. I cried. Sadie came to me in a dream. She said that happened so that I could have proof that animals did empathically absorb physical illness along with emotional energy. She also said that this, too, was a pre-life agreement we made together.

Her job was to keep me safe and to heal my physical issues so I could do what I was meant to do, which is help people heal with their pets. She taught me so much, and she still does. When she was getting ready to pass, with tears in my eyes, I asked her why she had to leave. I begged her not to go. She told me that she had done what she came to do, and it was time for her to move out of the way so another dog could come to me—a dog that wanted to be a service dog and be out in public. She said it was time for me to welcome that dog into my life.

I couldn't even think about another dog at that point. However, I did want to have a dog that liked going out and was gentler with everyone all the time. That made me feel guilty too. My Sadie could be aggressive and did not like to go places. She was always skeptical of new people. She said that was her job and I don't need that anymore. I needed a dog that would do healing work with me and others—this was my calling, and I was ready!

When Sadie Left My Physical World

The lessons are unbelievable and I've been learning a lot from Sadie after her passing. She died from advanced kidney disease at the age of 14. It was not a coincidence that I have had chronic bladder infections most of my life. I have maybe had only one or two since she passed in 2017. I rescued this precious girl when she was a puppy. Dr. Downey would call her "my special needs girl," and she was. She came to me with neurological trauma. She came to help me heal from my neurological imbalance, physical trauma, and to protect me from others. I wish I had known about Energetic Communication™ and neural restructuring then. She has helped me turn those low vibration emotions into gratitude for her teachings.

She had told me she wanted to die at home, with me. She also didn't want to leave until she knew I would be ok. I slept downstairs with her during her end-of-life because she could not get up the stairs anymore. I gave her IV fluids and hand-fed her. We had an amazing connection that I'll never forget. She would get into the cutest positions with her stuffed animals and her dog friend, Bella. I took the best pictures of her during her end-of-life transition. She wanted me to have pictures of her that made me feel happy. And they did.

She started to have seizures, and being the mama, I needed to make the decision to bring her to Dr. Downey for help transitioning. It was so hard, and I was grateful to have someone who knew and loved her throughout her life to help me.

After her passing, all my guilt for the things I thought I did wrong or didn't do right came flooding into my mind and emotions. I felt guilty because I had a trained professional do laser therapy to help heal her kidneys. It seemed like she went down quickly after that. I was worried that I made the wrong decision. And then she told me it was part of our pre-life plan. I needed to understand the grounding technique, Earthing, that I learned because of meeting the laser therapy professional. It has been a wonderful tool that has helped me a lot. So that is why Sadie brought her to me through her illness. If she was not sick, I would never have met this person and learned this remarkable tool.

Soon after she passed, I got a cold sore on my lip, and when I looked in the mirror—it was shaped like a perfect heart! I started crying because I knew it was Sadie telling me she was okay and she loved me.

I struggled with thinking this was all in my head and that I just wanted to see the heart. I did have others confirm that they saw a heart too. I decided to allow myself to believe that it was real and Sadie was communicating with me. *I have learned that there are no coincidences—they are messages if we choose to believe.* They are messages to us from the Spirit world. They are messages from our loved ones. When I chose to believe, I started to get a lot more coincidences in my life.

After a bit, I went into meditation and to my sacred space to connect with Sadie. Sierra, the dog I had before Sadie, was there. I looked around for Sadie, and then she ran out to me. She knew it was me. Sadie and Sierra ran to each other and blended and became a big beautiful white light full of love. This light, they said, was the next dog coming into my life. It was Ladybug, and she is the perfect blend of Sierra and Sadie! She came to me about three months after Sadie passed.

> *I am ok now and I was able to heal faster than I thought because of her teaching in this world and beyond. I still cry sometimes, only now I can also feel her love and I laugh at the silly things she would do. I realized that this, too, was a gift from her. I grew to understand that we need to have maintenance cries to let the physical goo of stress in our bodies out. Sadie and Sierra help me cry when I need to, and I appreciate it.*

Siera

Sadie

Bella & Sadie

WILD ANIMAL STORIES

The Chicks

I went to Maine with some friends to their campground. We visited some other friends down the road who had a farm with chickens. The hens called me over to do some healing on them. I used the HESU™ Tool, Tuning Forks, and Image-Emotion Sets™ for their health and wellbeing.

The next day, I was informed that three hens had not been laying eggs. However, that day, there was a commotion in the chicken coop, and low and behold, the ladies had all laid eggs. You go, girls!

The Chicks!

Testosterone Imbalanced Rhinoceros

In 2021, I started doing healing for the animals at the local zoos. I had been called for several years by the animals to do this and just never found the time—so this was the time. First, I connected with the animals at the Stone Zoo in Stoneham, MA, in meditation. A rhinoceros contacted me and was very upset. They said that their testosterone needed to be balanced and that they were afraid they would hurt their mate. They said they knew they were not acting right; however, they did not know how to change and wanted my help. Well, I thought that this would be interesting.

I went to the zoo for my first of many healing trips to come. I fully expected to see a rhinoceros walking through the zoo—but I did not see any. I was very confused and thought it was probably just in my head or perhaps at another zoo.

As my partner and I started walking through the bird area, we heard a commotion. My partner told me I was needed. I had my gemstones and tuning forks and was using the HESU™Tool on each animal along our path. When I turned the corner, I saw what he was talking about.

There were two Hornbill birds in an enclosure. One of them (I assumed was the male) was grabbing the other by her bill and throwing her around. He kept doing this and the female was begging me to help. I immediately sat down, and for the next half hour or more, I provided clearing, balancing, and healing for both of them. The male finally admitted he did not know what to do and he did not want to hurt his mate. It sure sounded like the message I had gotten from the rhinoceros; however, these were Hornbill birds.

I realized that he needed his DNA repaired, and because he was in captivity, he had not learned the proper way to woo his mate. I did some neural restructuring and repaired his DNA. I put in a snippet of the correct way to woo his beautiful mate. I started sending Image-Emotion Sets™ of the snippet of him feeding his mate and not throwing her across their enclosure. He had become confused in his "excitement" and was willing to learn.

He finally stopped and just stared at me, like he realized I was the one he had asked for help. I kept providing healing for his mate as her nerves were frazzled—and that was understandable. I had to reprimand him at times to "shake" him out of his reign of terror, and he finally got it.

He looked at me and tilted his head. He jumped down and picked up some food with his beak. I was so excited... yes, yes, I told him, that is great. I fully expected him to jump back up and feed his mate. Instead, he gulped it down and then jumped up and stood quietly next to his mate. Well, it was a start, I thought—baby steps. He was not throwing her around anymore.

Over the next year, I continued to visit them and provide clearing, balancing, and healing work for them, hoping to see some babies. About the third time I went, my partner pointed out the sign by their enclosure—*Rhinoceros Hornbills!* He was my rhinoceros! I never took the time to read their actual names.

I found my rhinoceros, and they have not bred, as far as I know; however, perhaps you would be willing to use the HESU™ Tool with intentions for them to have little Rhinoceros Hornbills in the near future?

Rhinoceros Hornbill's

Humpback Whales

I decided to go on a meditative journey to the ocean and see who would come to see me. I was curious about what messages they might have. I saw turtles (my main Spirit Animal), dolphins, different colored fish, squids, and so many more friends. They all just swam by. After a bit of swimming around, I felt a rush of water through my body. I then saw a huge Humpback whale coming toward me, she swam right up to me and looked me straight in the eyes with her amazingly big eye. I felt a little intimidated. I asked her what her name was and if she had any messages for me. She made an interesting sound, which I presumed was their name, and then I got an image of water currents. She told me to come along as she had to show me something.

She told me that Humpbacks are the ambassadors of the ocean, and they were struggling because Antarctica was burning. I didn't understand. The whale took me to where the Fukushima Daiichi nuclear accident occurred in Japan. At the time, I didn't know what this was and had to Google it. It's known as The Great East Japan Earthquake with a magnitude of 9.0 that happened at 2:46 p.m. on Friday, March 11, 2011. It did considerable damage in the region, and the large tsunami it created caused a lot more.

My friend (the Humpback whale) told me that warm water was flowing through a crack at the bottom of the ocean, which she showed me. She said that the sea water was being used to cool the "reactors," and then it was flowing back into the ocean warmer than before. This, she said, was causing the currents to change and the ice to melt in Antarctica, which caused a reduction in their food supply and the death of younger whales. I really did not know how to find out if this was true. There were no reports that I could find that mentioned how they were cooling the reactors. I certainly didn't know who to tell that would take me seriously and not think I was crazy! I did reach out in an email to a Boston Aquarium Marine Biologist. As I expected, I did not get a response back. I had to sit on this information, and it has really bothered me. If someone reading this book can find this out and do something about it, we would really appreciate it! Please reach out and let me know what you find.

The Bees Have Needs

I was called to do a meditation to talk with the bees. I'm allergic to bees, so I was curious what their message was going to be. When I connected with them, they took me on a ride. As we were flying around, I kept getting hit with sticky fuzz balls. The bees showed me how they see and identify the right flowers to pollinate. It was amazing at first, but then I noticed that the more we flew, the less I could see the right color flowers for them to pollinate. The fuzz balls were sticking to my face and eyes and changing the colors I was seeing. The bees said this is what was happening to them too.

I asked them what these fuzz balls were. They flew me to a place they said was really bad in hopes that I could figure it out. They brought me to a row of high-voltage transmission lines. The buzz from those lines was loud, and I could see the fuzz balls coming off them. The bees showed me cell phone towers and underground wires that were all causing these fuzz balls and they said that it was getting worse. The bees said that the fuzz balls would stick to them, and then when they went into their hive, the fuzz balls would get all over their food and babies and eventually kill their queen.

Holy Bees, what the heck! We have to do something!

After doing some research, I came to believe that the fuzz balls were electromagnetic fields (EMFs). I found out that they were bothering me too, and I needed to ground myself more. I learned about Earthing from my dog Sadie, which is one way to ground. I did not know how to utilize this technology to help my bee friends. I remembered something a Microsoft tech person once told me—he said that before he could go into the big computer room, he had to hold a metal rod that extended into the earth to "ground" himself first, or he could short out the computers. It's like when we push the button on the elevator and get shocked. Simply put, this is discharging the EMF build-up via grounding.

I wondered if this could work for the bees. They needed a grounding rod or something that they could land on to discharge the EMF buildup, so they did not bring it into their hives. Something to clean themselves off by discharging the energy and grounding themselves. This may not be a solution for the bigger EMF problem; however, it could help to sustain the bees' existence until we can figure out better solutions. I have told a few beekeepers with the hope that someone could test this theory and see if it could help save the bees.

Wild Animal Meditations

I created some meditations that you can use to help the wild animals. They would be forever grateful for your healing intentions for them. And so would we!

Use your camera to scan the QR code or follow the link to explore the information

13

CREATE YOUR ACTION PLAN

"Never be afraid to try something new. Remember, amateurs built the Ark. Professionals built the Titanic!" - Anonymous

love that quote! It is so true. I have, in the past, held myself back from doing the things I love because I did not think I was good enough. I did not have the degree or certification, and I was still making mistakes.

I still do not feel like an expert in Energetic Communication™. I learn new things all the time and make plenty of mistakes. As an intuitive language, it can be misinterpreted at times. I have been frustrated and have found it difficult to stay in high vibration emotions when things are not changing as quickly or in the way I want.

Energetic Communication™ is a new language that Ladybug and I are introducing. I believe there will be parts that resonate and are easy for some and not for others. For those who have difficulty visualizing, no worries your pets will help you learn.

As with any new language, it will take some time to get comfortable "speaking" it. The more we dive in and consistently work with the tools and concepts, the easier it gets. Once we become confident, these tools will become quick and easy to use. They will become maintenance tools we can use to keep our pets healthy, happy, and safe.

I encourage people to keep a journal of what they do and any changes they notice in their pets. Note even very small changes or responses, like looking at us differently or noticing when we are using the HESU™ Tool or one of the other tools. Maybe they simply change the way they walk to the door or when they go to bed. Just be curious and aware.

Use these tools for three months before deciding to keep or toss them. The life of a red blood cell is 90-120 days—so our pets will have had plenty of renewal and exposure for us to know if the tools are helping.

Always make sure any concerning physical or behavioral changes in pets that occur suddenly are checked by a veterinarian ASAP. Some examples can include stopping eating or drinking for more than one day, vomiting more than twice, peeing or pooping in the house, or new aggressive or sleepy behavior. Note: They may be more tired because of the energy shifting in their bodies; however, it should not be a dramatic shift. If in question, a veterinarian should be consulted.

As needed, please seek help from specialists such as a holistic veterinarian, pet psychic-medium, behavioral therapist, pet flower essence expert, nutritionist, and trainer.

LET'S CREATE YOUR ACTION PLAN.

Learning to use all the tools can be overwhelming. Let them naturally come up in your thoughts, and do them as you are called.

I recommend starting with the HESU™ Tools because they clear, balance, and provide healing for our pets. Then, let the rest of them happen over the next three months. For those of you who like a plan, I have outlined one below.

Harmonic Energetic Set-Up (HESU)

Use this tool as much as possible during the first month. Then, once a day is usually sufficient. Use it more during times of increased stress, meeting new people or animals, leaving one place for another, and when they are sick or injured.

Foundation: daily

- Ground, Connect, Filter
- Clear, Balance, Heal
- A river forms around them, separating their energy from ours and all others.

During times of increased stress, working to change behaviors, or improving health, there is no limit to using this tool. Use it as much as possible and keep it simple

Start with the HESU Foundation and then add these:

For you: daily for the first month, then during stress, say:

- I call my energy that you have absorbed back to me.
- I return your energy that I have absorbed from you back to you.

- All energy is cleared, balanced, and healed for the Highest Good of All.
- The River of Possibilities flows between us.

For others, including other pets and animals, say:

- Return all (your pet's name) energy that is not theirs back to where it belongs.
- Return all (your pet's name) energy back to them.
- All energy is cleared, balanced, and healed for the highest good of all.
- The River of Possibilities flows between them and all others.

Image-Emotion Sets™

Ladybug and I suggest using the "go-to" **Image-Emotion Sets™** to begin with. These are the ones that were created in Chapter Four.

I outlined them below. Visualize and feel them every day and throughout the day. Look at the pictures one at a time for 30 seconds or more, and then look at the other.

1. Find a picture of your pet when they look cute, happy, and feel safe.
   - How does that picture make you feel?
   - Spend 30 seconds looking at this picture and feeling the high vibration emotions that it brings up for you.
2. Find a picture where your pet is looking happy, confident, and healthy.
   - How does this picture make you feel?
   - Spend 30 seconds looking at this picture and feeling the high vibration emotions that it brings up for you.

When you gain confidence in using your "go-to" **Image-Emotion Sets™**, you can start creating more. Some examples are how we want our pets to behave and what we want them to know. Creating images of what you want your relationship to look like and how you want your pets to respond to situations is very powerful. Remember that these behaviors probably have a neural network and have become more of a reactional pattern. It will take time to change them and may need **Neural Restructuring** to change.

The more **Image-Emotion Sets™** we create and use over time, the stronger our communication is received by our pets.

When you are feeling old fears, anger, worries, frustrations, and anxieties, it is important to feel them. Then go directly to the **Image-Emotion Sets™** you've already created. Your go-to **Image-Emotion Sets™** are wonderful to use when you feel stuck in the low vibration emotions. Our pets will respond to the higher vibration emotions of joy, gratitude, peace, confidence, etc., over the low vibrational emotions. That means our pets will be able to see the image of what we want them to do and feel the emotions that will encourage them to do it. They will ignore the original low vibration emotions. Soon, the **Image-Emotion Sets™** we create will string together and form a wonderfully high vibration intuitive language. Add the gemstones and chakra healing tools, and you are on the right track to "speaking" Energetic Communication™.

GEMSTONES AND CHAKRA HEALING

Use this tool daily for a week and then when you feel your pets want it. You'll start receiving your pet's **Image-Emotion Sets™**. When we receive an image of using the gemstones on them, and it feels good, then it is them "talking" to us. It could be a message from our pet that they want us to use that tool on them.

Make sure to clear and charge your gemstones in salt water for five minutes or longer before the first time and always after use.

We can use the tools on ourselves, too. I encourage everyone to see what it's like. We may find them very helpful. Create an action plan for yourself, too!

Healing Pet

We can start the gemstone healing for our pets using a Healing Pet surrogate to help them adjust to the high vibrations of healing we are providing. We can make our own Healing Pet with chakras and colors like our pets. It's a fun activity to do with the family.

Pet Communication and Healing Toolkit

I have created this complete Webinar in a charming bag to provide more guidance and instruction for you to create and work with your Healing Pet. All the materials are included. The Healing Pet is made of linen, sewed with cotton thread, and stuffed with natural organic cotton and goose down.

Pet Communication Toolkit Instructional Video

Use your camera to scan the QR code to explore the information

Spirit Animals

If we want to open the door to amazing and magical relationships, we can invite our pet's Spirit Animals to come and play. They are fun and powerful – all they need is an invitation. They bring us high vibration energy and can help us find solutions we had not thought of.

Spirit Animal Message Toolkit

I have created this complete Webinar in a charming bag for those who want more guidance and to dive deeper into the magical and transformative world of Spirit Animal Guides and Friends!

Spirit Animal Message Toolkit Instructional Video

Use your camera to scan the QR code to explore the information

Ladybug and I thank you for exploring **Energetic Communication™** with us. We hope you have found the information helpful and will enjoy using the tools with your pets.

We would love your feedback! Let us know how the tools worked or didn't work for you and your pets. Stories about you and your pets' experiences are the best. We love to hear from you, so please share.

There is a lot of information, tools, and perspectives that have been provided and it may be overwhelming. Remember you are learning a new language, so take it slow and have patience.

If you would like more guidance, Ladybug and I would be honored to help. There are many ways we can work together and we are happy to work with you to develop these tools and incorporate them more effectively for your unique needs.

Pet Talk & Tool Program

We hope you enjoy our full Pet Program with fabulous webinars, animations, videos, meditations, and other resources from our library of resources!

Use your camera to scan the QR code to explore the information

MY SERVICES AND OFFERINGS

Private Sessions

- Single Sessions
- Month Mentoring Program
- Three-Month Mentoring Program

Classes, Webinars, and Events

- Pet Communication & Healing
- More HESU™ Tools
- Spirit Animal Reiki Class
- Usui Holy Fire® III Reiki Classes

   o   Level I, II, and Master

Complete Workshops in a Charming Bag

- Pet Communication & Healing Toolkit
- Spirit Animal Messages Toolkit

Meditations

- Moon Cycle Healing
- Equinox/Solstice Manifesting Cycle
- Journey With Your Spirit Animals and Guides

Field Trips

- Zoo—Healing the Ambassadors with Gratitude
- Healing the Wild Animals and Their Land
- Ceremonies for Healing with Mother Earth

Patti Anastasia
&
Ladybug

May Everything Always Be Better Than Your Expect!

Thank you for taking the time to read our book. We hope you found it helpful and are excited to explore all the wonderful information, tools, and resources we have brought to you and your beloved companions!

If you are able to provide a review, it would mean the world to me and Ladybug. Your voice helps us grow and improve, and we are deeply grateful for your contribution.

Use your camera to scan this QR Code to visit our website or go to where you purchased this book, and let us and others know what you think!

Your feedback is invaluable to us. 🙏❤️🐞

CLIFF NOTES

1. **Akashic Records** – I call them the Spiritual Internet. All that has happened, will happen, and is currently happening in our and parallel worlds can be accessed through intuitive language here.

2. **Analogy of The Rainforest** – The filtration system we can create through intention with our pets to keep our and their energy cleared, balanced, and healed. Our pets absorb our toxins (rainforest), and we are the rain that cleanses them and creates a healthy and healed energy flow between us. Together, we can heal the world (oxygen).

3. **Animal Communication** – The ability to receive and send messages to and from animals.

4. **Ascend** – Out-of-body experience by traveling to the higher dimensions either consciously or transitioning through death.

5. **Ascended Masters** – Those who have lived in the physical world as Spiritual Leaders can ascend and descend at will to continue helping us to balance Karma and transmute Legacy.

6. **Auric Field** – The energetic field surrounding our bodies is fueled by our chakras and moon beam energy. It is also one of our filters.

It acts as a magnet to pull our Life Purpose Paths to us. The higher the frequency, the more Life Purpose Healing Paths we draw to us.

7. **Chakra Centers** – Wheels of energy are represented by colors and associated with specific regions in our bodies. Seven chakra wheels/centers in our body are connected to particular emotions, organs, and Spiritual attributes.

8. **Chakra Healing** – Working with the body's chakras to clear, balance, and set them for the highest good. Aligning them to create a powerful and healing flow of energy through the body will assist in manifesting health, wealth, and happiness.

9. **Core Energy** – Our pure energy without any empathic energy interference. We are Caring-Clear-Compassionate-Complete-Competent-Content-Considerate-Curious. **Currency** – The balance of giving and receiving in the physical world. It can take the form of emotional support, money, barter, and Spiritual growth.

10. **Currency** – The balance of giving and receiving in the physical World. It can take the form of emotional support, money, barter, and Spiritual growth.

11. **Dark Night of The Soul** – A time in a human's life when they become stuck in the low vibration emotions to the point where hope is lost. This is usually caused by severe loss in our lives. Thoughts of suicide or complete detachment from others can occur. This time is meant to completely change the direction we are taking in our lives to better align with our Life Purpose. When this happens, we need the help of others to regain our strength and make the changes necessary to regain our joy and re-align with our Life Purpose Healing Paths.

12. **DNA Balancing** – The process by which the DNA structure is cleared, balanced, and healed following Neural Restructuring for change to become permanent.

13. **End-Of-Life Process** – Begins with palliative care and progresses through transitioning of the Soul, and ends with completion of the grieving cycle.

14. **Energetic Communication™** – Made up of three tools—Harmonic Energetic Set-Up™, Image-Emotion Sets™, and High Vibrational Healing Tools. They improve and add to our psychic and intuitive abilities to provide healing and to talk with our pets.

15. **Essential Oils** – Concentrated plant extracts that retain the natural smell and flavor of their source. They are used to help specific concerns when used as a scent, applied to skin, or ingested. *CAUTION—When using them with animals, one must have advanced training to understand how to mix and what is appropriate for a specific species. Never use an infuser in homes with animals as the mist can be accidentally inhaled, ingested through food or water, or irritate their eyes, and may cause illness, allergic reaction, and possible death.* Check out flower essences for a safer alternative.

16. **Fight or Flight Response** – When the sympathetic nervous system is triggered in response to danger, for survival, and or safety.

17. **Flower Essences** – Created using the various parts of a flower blossom and made into liquid extracts. We can use them to address profound issues of emotional well-being, soul development, and mind-body health. First developed in the 1930s by an English physician, Dr. Edward Bach. He prepared 38 remedies, mostly

from English wildflowers. In recent decades more have followed in his footprints. They work amazingly well for our pets and animals.

18. **Gemstones** – I call all stones and crystals gemstones because they are all gems to me!

19. **Grief Cycle** – Five stages of grief cycle: denial, anger, bargaining, depression, and acceptance. Not necessarily in that order.

20. **Grief Loop** – When we get stuck in the grief cycle and continue to relive the five stages of grief over and over again, usually, it is because we are feeling guilty about something we believe we did wrong or could have done better.

21. **Harmonic Energetic Set-Up™** –A system I downloaded from the spirits that keeps us in our core energy and protects us from empathic energy that is not for our highest good.

22. **Healing Maintenance** – Using quick and easy tools to keep us and our pets clear and balanced while also providing healing, protection, and manifesting.

23. **Healing Pet** – Surrogate stuffed animals or items we can use to provide healing for animals that are not ready for, or we cannot touch.

24. **HESU™ Tool** – Foundation tool of the Harmonic Energetic Set-Up™ that is used to clear, balance, and provide healing for us, animals, and the world.

25. **High Vibrational Field** – The vibrational frequency that surrounds us and interacts with our aura. It magnetizes High Vibration Life Healing Paths for us to choose from. It can be damaged with low vibration energy.

26. **High Vibrational Frequencies** – The frequencies associated with high vibration emotions and tools.

27. **High Vibrational Healing Tools** – Energetic tools create a high vibrational healing frequency that helps promote healing for us and our pets.

28. **Holy Fire and Violet Flame Filter** – Outer filter set with intention to transmute all energy we release and receive for the highest good of all—especially for us.

29. **Human Experience** – The experience that we planned to have prior to entering a specific lifetime. Supports our karmic path.

30. **Human Job** – The physical job we do that brings us the currency we need to prosper in our current lifetime.

31. **Image-Emotion Sets™** - Visualizations paired with the most intense emotions associated. The "parts" of speech of the Universal Language.

32. **Karma** – Our original intention for what we will heal in the physical World is to create more love. The path of all our lifetimes. Karma is to be balanced by clearing legacy.

33. **Karmic Destiny** – The specific path we choose in collaboration with others for a current lifetime.

34. **Karmic-Legacy Pet** *– Strong Spiritual relationship with certain pets.* We plan to connect in our current lifetime for a specific reason at a certain time. These relationships teach us that there is more beyond this lifetime.

35. **Karmic Skills** – The skills we learned in past lifetimes that we bring into our current lifetime. They are our natural abilities.

36. **Legacy** – The genetics, belief systems, and trauma of our current and past lifetimes. This is what can block or propel the balancing of karma and can cause disruption in our current lifetime.

37. **Legacy Roots** – Genetic and inherited energy caused by past traumas that are expressed in our current lifetime and need to be transmuted.

38. **Life Purpose** – Why we came into the physical World—our Karmic path. We can only experience it through the paths we choose, and we cannot say or know exactly what it is.

39. **Life Purpose Paths** – The paths we take in life that led us in the direction of our Life Purpose.

40. **Life Purpose Healing Paths** – The paths we walk that are perfectly in line with our Spirit and human jobs. They fill us with joy. When all the paths we walk in life are these, we are living our Life Purpose.

41. **Low Vibrational Emotions** – Emotions that are contracting and dense. Emotions that are approximately in the 0-175 Hz range. Examples: Shame, guilt, depression, grief, fear, jealousy, rage, and worry.

42. **Low Vibrational Frequency** – The frequencies, as measured by Hz, that break down our Auric Field.

43. **Maintenance Cry** – As we change through growth, pain, and opportunities, our bodies need to release the residue from these things for us to fulfill our Life Purpose in our current Lifetime. This is one important way we can do that. Our pets that have passed can give us this gift throughout our lives by helping us cry.

44. **Medium** – A person who can directly talk with disembodied Spirits. This ability allows one to talk with animals too.

45. **Meridian System** – Based on the Chinese Acupuncture system. It is made up of six paired meridian flows represented by Yin and Yang energies to make up 12 meridians in total. Each meridian is named for the organ system it governs. Each meridian runs along a neural network.

46. **Moonbeam Filter** – Inner filter set with intention that surrounds us and is energized with the moon's energy. It magnetizes our Life Purpose Healing Paths to us, and assists in transmuting Legacy. Also called our Auric Field.

47. **Mother Earth Healing Stones** – These are the stones we set an intention for healing and ask Mother Earth to show us their power and then stroke our pets with them.

48. **Neural Restructuring** – The energetic "clipping" of PTSD neural pathways that are causing a trigger reaction from past trauma. They are replaced with healthy responses.

49. **Neural Rut** – The PTSD neural pathways form and become deeper and stronger with continued stimulus, causing an ingrained reaction. They become a patterned reaction that will need to be retrained when a behavior change is the desired outcome following Neural Restructuring.

50. **Palo Santo** – Used for clearing, balancing, and connecting with high vibration Spirits and guides by smudging our Auric Field and spaces. It comes from a wild tree native to South America, and

its scientific name is *Bursera graveolens*, which translates to "holy wood."

51. **Personal Life Force Energy** – The energy that fuels our physical and Spiritual bodies in our current lifetime. It carries our Karmic Skills, tools, and the struggles we came to learn from. It depletes with age, illness, and lack of conscious regeneration time.

52. **Pet Communication and Healing Toolkit** – Contains all the materials needed to create a Healing Pet. Includes full instruction, gemstones, guided meditations, chakra chart, and videos on how to use it.

53. **Pet Goals** – What our pets want to teach us about ourselves, like our natural skills and how we are special.

54. **Pet Jobs** – What our pets do for us and are their healthy and natural skills. They would be doing these jobs in their natural environment if they were not domesticated.

55. **Pet Messages** – What our pets are telling us about what our healthy and natural skills are with their behaviors, illness, and by mirroring us.

56. **Pet Palliative Care Cycle: Care and Comfort** – The shift in the focus to care-to-comfort measures and not curing disease processes that we can provide for our pets as they age.

57. **Pet Psychic-Medium** – A person who talks with animals and uses intuition to determine certain emotional and physical causes for illness and behaviors. They can convey messages pets have for their pet parents.

58. **Pre-Life Plan** – The plan we form with others and animals in the Spirit world before entering a current lifetime to fulfill our Karmic Destiny.

59. **Psychic** – A person that can naturally access the Akashic Records to gain insight into a specific person, pet, or event through time and space.

60. **React** – A triggered action taken or spoken automatically and instantly without thought.

61. **Reiki** – The word Reiki is made of two Japanese words—Rei, which means "God's wisdom or the Higher Power," and Ki, which is "life force energy." So, Reiki is actually "spiritually guided life force energy. Reiki is a pseudoscientific practice based on metaphysical concepts. Developed in the 1920s by Mikao Usui in Japan, it is a technique used for stress reduction and relaxation that can also promote healing. It is administered by "laying on hands" and is based on the idea that an unseen "life force energy" flows through us and is what causes us to be alive.

62. **Resonant Frequency** – The natural frequency where something or someone vibrates at the highest vibrational frequency without amplification from another source.

63. **Respond** – A thoughtful action taken or spoken in time after consideration of outcomes.

64. **River of Possibilities** – The space created with intention outside of our filters that separates us from all others and things. It keeps us in our core energy and not empathically absorbing others energy or giving away ours. It is also known as the *Universal Life Force Energy*. It creates the space between us all that sets boundaries and allows

our guides to "drop" surprises, opportunities, and what we want to manifest into our lives.

65. **Sage** – The person we become as we walk our Life Purpose Healing Paths. It is the balance of our Spirit Jobs with our Human Jobs that creates currency in our physical lives by using our natural gifts and learned skills. We experience pure joy in our lives as we become a Sage. (Also, a plant that is burned in a cleansing "smudging" ritual).

66. **Soul/Spirit Point** – Located at our navel and can be thought of as our umbilical cord connecting our Soul to our Spirit and Source. The energetic flow is in both directions and facilitates all transitions in life. It can restore our life force energy and is used with our intention for healing and release. It can also be used as a point of transition from physical to Spirit worlds and back. It is utilized during ascension and descension.

67. **Spirit Animal** – Animals in our physical and Spiritual worlds that act as guides to deliver important messages, protection, and assist us with manifesting when called upon.

68. **Spirit Guides** – Animals, loved ones, Ascended Masters, Spirit Animals, angels, Council of Nine, and all helpers we request that are in Spirit and not physical form to guide us.

69. **Spirit Jobs** – The natural skills and abilities we have learned in past Karmic lives that we have experienced and brought into our current lifetime to help us. It must be worked consciously in time with a willingness to effect change and provide healing for the world and others.

70. **Spirit Animal Messages Toolkit** – Contains all the materials needed to connect with a specific Spirit Animal through gemstones, guided meditations, videos, and manifesting grid and candle. Includes full instructions on how to use it.

71. **Spirit Animal Reiki Classes** – A two-day class that connects us through symbols placed into our Soul bodies by specific Spirit Animals. After receiving these symbols, other animals in our physical world, in our dream state, and in meditation bring us messages, offer direction for our actions, and give us gifts.

72. **Spirit Animal Specialists** – Will assist us upon request for a certain time to help us with specific intentions of healing, meeting the right people to solve issues, completing projects, and for protection.

73. **Spiritual Leaders** – Those who remember how to connect with the Spiritual world at will and have a mission to help others find their Life Purpose Healing Paths.

74. **Spiritual Relationship** – A relationship we can form with our deceased pets and others in the Spirit world. We can gain knowledge, guidance, and healing through their high vibration frequencies and love.

75. **Talking Feather** – A native American (Nations) tradition used in group counsel, planning, and grievances to set the boundary for expression of one without interruption from others until the feather is passed. Those holding the feather have the floor during discussions until the feather is passed to the next person.

76. **The Perfect Empath** – Animals empathically absorb energy from us and others completely without intention, thought, or desire.

They are not able to clear, balance, and heal their energy alone and must work in unison with their pet parent to release the energy they have empathically absorbed.

77. **The Rainbow Bridge** – A process referred to as our pet's transition from the physical to the Spirit world. Can be assisted by others or occur naturally at their End-of-Life.

78. **Transition Cycle** – The time frame when we accept that our loved ones are leaving this world for the next. Body cells are collapsing, and the physical body is dying. It is complete when the Soul returns to its Source.

79. **Universal Language** – The unspoken intuitive language is made up of images and emotions—it is our animals' natural language. We all knew it as infants, and some have retained the ability as they grew into adults. Everyone can access this neural network and use it with training.

80. **Universal Life Force Energy** – The natural flow of energy that surrounds us and supports Spiritual balance and communication. The space between us and others where we can set our intention for manifesting into its currents. It is where we work our Spirit Jobs and can set energetic boundaries.

81. **Vibrational Frequencies** – All physical matter vibrates with a specific frequency and intensity at a given time in space. Matter can transmute into other forms of matter when another vibrational frequency interacts with it, creating a new resonant frequency.

QR CODES WITH LINKS

1. Meet The Authors
https://qr1.be/7RHH

2. Anna Breytenbach, Animal Communicator
https://qr1.be/WFMN

3. Harmonic Energetic Set-Up™ Program
https://qr1.be/K84X

4. Image-Emotion Set™ Webinar
 https://qr1.be/XJ3S

5. Cesar Millan – The Dog Wisper
https://qr1.be/CMQY

6. Diane Kazer at CHI Holistic Health Institute
https://qr1.be/KGM4

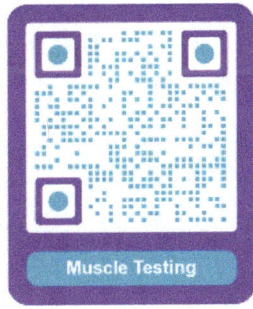

7. The National Center for Biotechnology Information (Human PTSD Mode) - https://qr1.be/EEXE

8. The National Center for Biotechnology Information (Animal PTSD Model) - https://qr1.be/6MNP

9. The National Park Service – Vibrational Frequencies
https://qr1.be/K75I

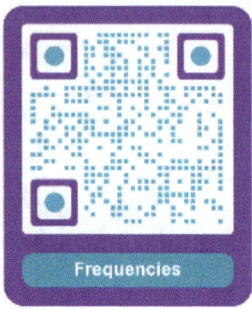

10. The Law of Resonance
https://qr1.be/HF5L

11. Kati Kaia – Vibrational Frequencies of Crystals
https://qr1.be/FY0H

12. Using Gemstone With Your Pets

https://qr1.be/ZEGA

13. Frequencies of Fabric

https://qr1.be/GLJZ

14. Meditations To Play For Your Pet

https://qr1.be/G37X

15. Spirit Pieces

https://qr1.be/49MF

16. Pet Grief & Loss Meditation Series

https://qr1.be/AI26

17. Connect with Your Lost Pet Meditations

https://qr1.be/3RY5

18. Wild Animal Meditations
https://qr1.be/HSPA

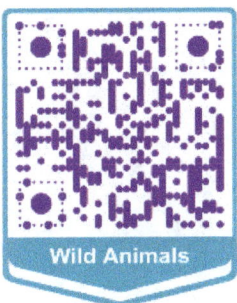

19. Pet Communication Toolkit Video
https://qr1.be/LXKR

20. Spirit Animal Message Toolkit Video
https://qr1.be/EWR3

21. Pet Talk & Tool Program

https://qr1.be/IMGE

22. My Website

www.YourAnimalHealer.com